PRAYING WI

Ava

Blessings
Joe Aldred

PRAYING WITH POWER

Edited by
BISHOP JOE ALDRED

CONTINUUM
London and New York

Continuum
The Tower Building, 11 York Road, London SE1 7NX
370 Lexington Avenue, New York, NY 10017-6503

© 2000 Centre for Black and White Christian Partnership

All rights reserved. No part of this publication may be reproduced or transmitted in any form or by any means, electronic or mechanical including photocopying, recording or any information storage or retrieval system, without prior permission in writing from the publishers.

Scripture quotations taken from the HOLY BIBLE, NEW INTERNATIONAL VERSION. Copyright © 1973, 1978, 1984 by International Bible Society. Used by permission of Hodder & Stoughton Ltd, a member of the Hodder Headline Plc Group. All rights reserved.

First published 2000

British Library Cataloguing-in-Publication Data
A catalogue record for this book is available from the British Library.

ISBN 0–8264–9984–0

Typeset by Kenneth Burnley, Wirral, Cheshire.
Printed and bound in Great Britain by
The Guernsey Press Co. Ltd, Guernsey, C.I.

CONTENTS

Introduction	vii
Steps to a successful prayer life *Don W. McFarlane*	1
Help! I can't pray *Delroy Hall*	14
Patience in prayer *Ron Brown*	25
Praying for a partner *Pall Singh*	35
A prayerful life *Hughes Redhead*	44
Becoming a handmaid of the Lord *Elizabeth Murove*	54
Prayer and decision-making *Cebert Richards*	67
Praying in the Spirit *Philip Mohabir*	77
Praying from the underside: breaking forth into liberation *Ronald A. Nathan*	90
Inter-generational conversations and prayer *Anthony Reddie*	102
Affirming God's sovereignty in coping with natural disaster: a Montserrat experience *Clarice Barnes and Ruthlyn Bradshaw*	119

Why write? Reflections through prayer   127
Hyacinth Sweeney

Prayer and fasting   146
Carl Smith

INTRODUCTION

After they prayed, the place where they were meeting was shaken. (Acts 4:31a, NIV)

Each one had a harp and they were holding golden bowls full of incense, which are the prayers of the saints. (Revelation 5:8b, NIV)

These two first-century prayer settings, one in a house in Jerusalem, the other somewhere in heaven, give us a sense of both the power and endurance qualities that have come to epitomise Christian – particularly black – attitudes toward prayer. This book brings together some reflections on prayer from a range of perspectives, from Christians who believe in both the power and eternal qualities of prayer. Some of these writers appeared in the 1998 publication, *Preaching with Power* (Cassell).

Editing these chapters has been a very enriching experience for me, as I have been challenged concerning my own prayer life. I am left pondering the various attempts by these writers to define and elaborate upon the prayer dynamic. Two main schools of thought emerge for me. First, there are those who embrace prayer as a *conversation*. For them, there is great significance in the two-way nature of a conversation: they both talk and listen to God. They need to converse regularly so that intimacy and empathy result. A kind of 'friend with friend' relationship evolves, aided by the Holy Spirit who acts as the medium or conduit: a kind of telephone, making communication possible. Second, there are those who embrace prayer as *power*. Here, prayer appears to be ascribed a life of its own: prayer is power and there is power in prayer! It is conceived as a God-given tool for the believer to utilize to break down the devil's strongholds and to take victory in any situation.

These two prayer positions appear to vie for supremacy in the Christian concept of what prayer is.

If I may, I will posit a third way on prayer, which emerges syncretistically from the conversation and power concepts in these chapters. I will call this, prayer as *authority*. In this model, the Christian communicates with God in the manner of an envoy abroad who, having received authority from his government through regular contact and counsel, acts in that power without the need for recourse to headquarters. So, Christians converse regularly, indeed constantly, with God, are clarified, instructed, energized and empowered from the contact, but take necessary action when needed without having to pray before they do. Prayer as *authority* brings both *conversation* and *power* together. Both are legitimate expressions of the Christian life as God's ambassadors in the world (1 Corinthians 5:20). There is an appropriate time to talk to God, and there is an appropriate time to talk directly to circumstances, principalities and powers in the authority God has given you already. However it is viewed academically and intellectually, prayer is of immense interest to most people: to Christians, people of other faiths, and to those of no faith. So this book comes as a tool to aid in the understanding of prayer. These writers have shared their heartfelt perspectives and pray that the reader be benefited.

Don McFarlane offers us a perspective on prayer as a privilege to enter into the throne-room of the King of the universe. For him, prayer is not an end in itself, but the means by which the believer enters the presence of God to ask and to receive. McFarlane shares ten steps in this prayer process to assist both the uninitiated and the seasoned pray-er.

Delroy Hall comes to the aid of those who feel that they just cannot pray. He offers some practical tips on how to overcome the 'I can't pray' dread. Hall emphasizes the need to understand prayer as a relationship with God through Jesus Christ that is aided by the Holy Spirit.

Ron Brown highlights the need for patience in prayer. Delay, he reminds us, is not denial. He argues that there is much to be valued in being made to learn to wait for that which is valuable. Brown suggests that in possessing their souls in patience, believers should wait, watch and worship: patience is not about idleness. He, along with others in this book, suggests that not least among the reason for some delays in Christians receiving that for which they pray, is their own slowness to change in conformity to God's will.

Pall Singh tackles the issue of praying for a partner. Here again, the imperative of patience is emphasized, against the danger of impulsiveness that often results in tears. Singh views prayer for life-partners as a communal activity, not just something for the unmarried. Combining prayer with action, he believes that there is a need for a closer cultural alliance between Asian concepts of arranged marriages and the West's emphasis upon individual choice.

Hughes Redhead posits prayer as the equivalent of breathing for the physical body, both in terms of its importance and its pervasive nature. He offers some advice to those who find it difficult to pray openly, but swiftly moves on to the perspective that prayer is much more than an activity: it is life. Redhead provides a list of biblical examples of a life of prayer, as opposed to prayer as mere activity, although he allows for the activity as part of the life.

Elizabeth Murove provides the reader with a model of intercessory praying: putting the needs of others above her own. However, this is not a detached intercessory approach. Murove both prays and engages with those for whom she prays: individuals, groups and whole countries. Hers is a personal testimony of prayerfully following God's instructions to intercede and minister to needs. Her transition of 'triumph' as the make of her motor car into a title for mission is powerful.

Cebert Richards takes us on a journey in how prayer can and should be applied to Christian decision-making. He argues that God has a plan for the universe and for each individual, and that the Christian in prayer seeks to discover how those divine plans impact upon the decision at hand. Richards says that to make decisions in God's will, the Christian must keep in close, prayerful touch with God.

Philip Mohabir makes a strong case for today's Church to rediscover the powerful prayer dynamic of the first-century Church. Their secret, he believes, was their close relationship with God through the Holy Spirit: their paraclete, divine helper and empowerer. Mohabir believes that intimacy with the divine is transforming, and he calls for a radical and revolutionary understanding of the role of the Holy Spirit in today's Church.

Ron Nathan brings to this discussion on prayer a clear Liberation Theology perspective. He teases the way in which prayer has been used codedly to cover up or highlight issues in the Black Church tradition. Much of what has been covered has been liberationist issues for oppressed people, such as racism, prejudice, inequalities, etc. Nathan examines the difference between the controlled public praying and passionate liberationist private praying that happens in the home. He calls for prayer to be used as a tool for the liberation of all oppressed people.

Anthony Reddie shares a piece of his PhD research into educational issues that affect children, particularly as these are mediated through the idiom of oral traditions. His chapter offers insights into the different perspectives on prayer held by the different generations in the familial network. Reddie shows how prayer has been used by black people as a concrete resource for surmounting struggles and achieving liberation, and as a tool for familial cohesion; and he makes a clear link between prayer and faith continuity in the family context.

Clarice Barnes and **Ruthlyn Bradshaw** are both from Montserrat and have experienced the traumas of the volcanic devastation of their island. They share insightfully and movingly how prayer has been applied to a situation of contested faith in an all-powerful God in an apparently powerless context. Barnes and Bradshaw show that early-morning meetings and other expressions of prayer became integral to the coping strategy of Christian Montserratians as they wrestled with questions about why God was permitting such catastrophe and where he was in their time of trouble.

Hyacinth Sweeney provides a rhetorical piece of work that takes the reader on a journey that explores how prayer influences her writing. She uses poetry as the main outcome of her prayerful wrestling with issues that concern her. Sweeney's poems are refreshingly frank in expressing her feelings, and they emerge as poignant outcomes of a complex journey.

Carl Smith links prayer with fasting and, later, worship as indispensable Christian disciplines. Using the Psalms as a resource, he shows the depth of prayer representation in these writings, as they present human attempts to engage a sovereign God. Smith gives limited credence to model prayers, arguing that such limitations are unhelpful when attempting to plumb the depths of God's resources and human need. He posits fasting as the tool whereby the Christian gains mastery over 'things' and self.

It is my hope that the passion with which prayer is believed in and practised by black Christians in Britain will come alive for the reader.

The project would not have happened without the administrative support of Donna Gordon-Rowe. She has given her time and talents as a volunteer at great cost to herself. We all owe her the uttermost gratitude. Donna has given herself in this way because she believes in the project. Once again, a big 'Thank you!'. Appreciation is due also to Nicola Balkham at the Centre office and Colleen Laing who helped us out at the end. All the contributors have done their work as a labour of love, and I thank them on all our behalfs for enriching our lives with their words.

Enjoy! Stay blessed!!

Bishop Joe Aldred
Executive Director
Centre for Black and White Christian Partnership

March 2000

STEPS TO A SUCCESSFUL PRAYER LIFE

Don W. McFarlane

Pastor Don McFarlane currently serves as President of the South England Conference of Seventh-day Adventists. A native of Jamaica, he graduated from West Indies College (now Northern Caribbean University) with a BA in Theology in 1973 and subsequently an MA in Pastoral Studies from Andrew's University in Michigan, USA. He served as a pastor and evangelist in Kingston, Jamaica from 1973 to 1978, when he was invited to join the ministerial team of the Seventh-day Adventist Church in the United Kingdom.

Between 1978 and 1984 Pastor McFarlane was the minister of several Seventh-day Adventist Churches in Birmingham, the most notable being Handsworth and Camphill. He was elected to serve as General Secretary of the North British Conference of Seventh-day Adventists in 1984, and in 1985 was invited to the same position for the national church. Pastor McFarlane has been the President of the South England Conference of Seventh-day Adventist since 1991.

Despite having served as a church administrator for sixteen years, Pastor McFarlane thinks of himself first and foremost as a pastor. He enjoys preaching and believes that the values that the Christian faith has to offer are exactly those needed by British society at this time. His wife Mary is a social worker. Their marriage has been blessed with three children, Jodi, Melea and Mardon.

I was awoken at one o'clock in the morning by the nagging ring of the telephone. Who could be calling me at such an unsociable hour? I put the receiver to my ear, half expecting the caller, on hearing my slow, sleepy tones, to say, 'Sorry, wrong number.' 'I am calling from the Birmingham Children's Hospital. Will you come immediately to baptize a sick little baby who I am afraid might not make it to morning? His mother has requested that you come.' It was the voice of the Ward Sister.

I quickly came to my senses, dressed as fast as I could, and jumped into my old Peugeot 505. It took no more than fifteen minutes to drive from my home in Handsworth Wood to the hospital. By the time I got to the ward everything was ready for the baptism. Samuel was only weeks old. He seemed weak and was barely hanging on to life. His mother was keeping vigil by his bed, her eyes filled with tears.

The Ward Sister – who had witnessed many infant baptisms – must have wondered why I did not look or sound like a priest. I politely declined the use of the provisions that she had made for the baptism and declared, 'Samuel will not die.' I am not a believer in infant baptism but I believe in a God who answers prayer and who is able to turn a seemingly lost cause into a miraculous triumph.

'Samuel will not die.' That was a bold statement, but it was a statement under-girded by a simple faith that God would answer my prayer on Samuel's behalf. That very week the worldwide family of Seventh-day Adventist Christians, the fellowship to which I belong, was studying the young child Samuel in the Bible. I took that as a sign that God would hear the cry of his servant.

I asked the Ward Sister to leave me with the mother for a while. I then shared with this sad and disconsolate mother my belief that God would heal her son, and tried to comfort her with words from scripture. I lifted up my soul in prayer to the Almighty on Samuel's behalf and committed him to the care of his heavenly Father.

Seventeen years on, Samuel is a strapping young man, living evidence that there is power in prayer.

The pages of scripture are painted with dramatic evidence that prayer does work. 2 Chronicles 20 records one of the most beautiful prayers in the Bible and the dramatic manner in which it was answered. The combined army of the Moabites and Ammonites was massing on the borders of Judah. In panic, some men went to Jehoshaphat, King of Judah, and told him about the impending invasion. 'A vast army is coming against you from Edom, from the other side of the sea,' they said. Jehoshaphat knew that Judah did not have the resources to fight this large army. He proclaimed a fast and called the nation together for a prayer meeting. I doubt that any army general, prime minister or president would call a prayer meeting today in response to the threat of an invading army, but Jehoshaphat did.

In the special prayer meeting that took place, Jehoshaphat prayed a prayer which for some, including myself, is the most beautiful prayer in the Bible:

> O Lord, God of our fathers, are you not the God who is in heaven? You rule over all the kingdoms of the nations. Power and might are in your hand, and no-one can withstand you . . . If calamity comes upon us, whether the sword of judgment, or plague or famine, we will stand in your presence before this temple that bears your Name and will cry out to you in our distress, and you will hear and save us . . . We have no power to face this vast army that is attacking us. We do not know what to do, but our eyes are upon you. (2 Chronicles 20:6–12, NIV)

Through Jahaziel, a prophet, the Lord told Jehoshaphat, 'You will not have to fight in this battle. Take up your positions; stand firm and see the deliverance the Lord will give you.'

Following the prayer meeting, Jehoshaphat called for a song service. The army of the Moabites and Ammonites was advancing upon Judah. The men of Judah calmly stood in their place and sang, 'Give thanks to the Lord, for His love endures for ever' (2 Chronicles 20:21, NIV). What a scene that must have been! Looking on the seemingly defenceless men of Judah, the Moabites and Ammonites must have thought that the battle was already theirs. That optimism soon turned to panic and disaster as they, as if responding to a supernatural command, began attacking each other and did not stop until they had destroyed themselves.

> . . . When in faith we take hold of His strength, He will change – wonderfully change – the most hopeless, discouraging outlook, if it is our heavenly Father's will. (Morneau, 1997, p.16)

> There is no experience through which man is called to go but prayer is there as a helper, a comforter and a guide. (Bounds, 1994, p. 93)

Of course, individual accounts of answered prayer are not isolated experiences. They emerge from a life of prayer and a relationship with God. God is not like Santa Claus, who we occasionally call up to effect a miracle for us.

The rest of this chapter outlines a number of important steps which we must follow if we are to have a successful prayer life. They are not necessarily sequential. All the steps should be a reality in the life of a person at any given time, if they are to experience the continual joy of answered prayer.

Step 1: Believe in God

Every journey has a beginning, and belief in God is the first step in the journey towards a successful prayer life. 'Anyone who comes to God must believe that He [God] exists . . . ' (Hebrews 11:6, NIV).

We cannot prove scientifically the existence of God. This statement troubles many good Christians but it is true. While we cannot prove scientifically that God exists, the evidences for His existence are overwhelming. Can we prove scientifically that Sir Isaac Newton existed? 'Yes,' some might be quick to say, but can we really prove that he existed? There is a statue of him in the centre of Grantham. He is credited with the discovery of the Law of Action and Reaction, the Law of Gravity and the Principles of Calculus. He is thought of in many circles as history's greatest scientist. However, none of this is scientific proof that he existed. But we all believe that Sir Isaac Newton existed. The evidences for his existence are many. We have the accounts of those who saw him and several books that are attributed to him. We also enjoy the many benefits of his discoveries. Though we cannot prove scientifically that God exists, the evidences for His existence are more overwhelming than those for the existence of Isaac Newton.

We see God's handiwork in nature – in the intricate pattern of the rose and in the wonders of the human body. We see Him at work in the lives of others. We hear the testimonies of those who have encountered Him and we know what He has done in our lives. We see His word and will in scripture and, above all, we see

Him revealed in the historical Jesus. We also have the written records of those who encountered the historical Jesus.

Believing that God exists, that He is sovereign, all knowing, all seeing, all powerful, and at the same time a being of inexhaustible love, is the foundation for a meaningful prayer life. It takes less faith to believe in the existence of God, His creative power and redemptive acts than it does to believe in a world that evolved all on its own.

Step 2: Trust in God

Genuine belief in the existence of God and in His great attributes naturally leads to Step 2, which is trust in God. Trust is more than belief. 'The devils also believe, and tremble' (James 2:19, KJV), but they do not trust in God. Trusting God constitutes leaving our lives completely in His hands with total confidence that He will not fail us. This is one of the great lessons that Christians need to learn. When God is our Father and our lives are in His hand we need not become anxious about anything. He will fix everything for us. In Matthew 6:25–34 Jesus urged His hearers to trust God as their Father and not worry about anything.

Some years ago a group of visitors at the National Mint were told by a workman in the smelting department that if the hand is dipped in water, the molten metal might be poured from the ladle over the palm without burning it. 'Perhaps you would like to try it,' he said to a gentleman in the party. 'No thank you,' he replied, 'I prefer to take your word for it.' Turning to the man's wife he said, 'Perhaps, madam, you will make the experiment.' 'Certainly,' she replied. She then bared her arm and thrust it into a bucket of water, then held it out calmly while the hot metal was poured on it.

'You see,' said the workman to the gentleman, 'you believed, but your wife trusted.'

One of the best definitions of trust in God is that purportedly given by an Indian Chief. After listening to a missionary trying to explain to him and his people about trust in God, with deep insight and wisdom he explained to his people that to trust God was to 'lean upon Him with all your weight'.

Those who seek a successful prayer life must lean upon God with all their weight. They must commit their lives fully into God's hand. They must trust Him implicitly.

Step 3: Keep connected to Jesus

'If you remain in me and my words remain in you, ask whatever you wish, and it will be given you' (John 15:7, NIV). At conversion Jesus comes into our lives through the Holy Spirit. He becomes ours and we become His. This experience is not to be a one-off in which for an hour, a day or a week we experience a spiritual high as we come to know the wonders of the love of Jesus: it is an experience that must be maintained.

John 15:7 indicates how this experience is maintained. It is the result of feeding upon the word. The indwelling of Christ is not wholly a mystical experience. We receive Christ by receiving His word. As we feed upon the scriptures our minds are enlightened. We make conscious choices to obey Christ through His word, and His power enables us to obey.

When we are connected to Christ and feed upon His words our thoughts become closely identified with His words and His divine will, so that when we pray we do so in harmony with that divine will. Thus Jesus could say, 'If you remain in me and my words remain in you, ask whatever you wish and it will be given you.' 'If we live according to His word, every precious promise He has given will be fulfilled in us. Only as we live in obedience to His word can we claim the fulfilment of His promises' (White, 1994, p. 174).

Step 4: Pray in harmony with God's will

To some degree this has been addressed in Step 3 but is important enough to warrant its own space. As Jesus contemplated His impending death in the Garden of Gethsemane, His humanity was crushed by the weight of the sin of the world. His soul recoiled from the experience that would be His the following day. He wished there were another way for man's salvation to be achieved than by His dying on the cross. However, He knew that what was paramount was His Father's will.

> Going a little farther, he fell with His face to the ground and prayed, 'My Father, if it is possible, may this cup be taken away from me. Yet not as I will, but as you will . . . He went away a second time and prayed, 'My Father, if it is not possible for this cup to be taken away unless I drink it, may your will be done.' (Matthew 26:39, 42, NIV)

Prayer essentially is not to move the heart of God to accept our will and grant us our desires; it is to bring us in harmony with the will of God and help us accept that will. The act of one praying all night gives the impression that it takes a lot to move the heart of God or that He has to be appeased by such an action. God is a God of love. He knows what we need before we ask Him. Prayer is designed not so much to move *His* heart but *our* hearts. Sometimes it takes an entire night, several days or even months for our will to become aligned with His. When such an alignment takes place He can act mightily on our behalf.

Step 5: Confess and forsake sins

The psalmist David in Psalm 66:18 says, 'If I had cherished sin in my heart the Lord would not have listened; but God has surely listened and heard my voice in prayer.' In other words, if one is wilfully and knowingly pursuing a sinful path, the Lord will not listen to their prayer. He will not take one's prayer seriously.

David was speaking from the vantage point of experience. It seems that for a considerable period of time he had not prayed. Some Bible scholars believe that this sad state of affairs was in connection with his murder of Uriah and his adultery with Bathsheba, Uriah's wife. He went from day to day without making confession. He resisted the prompting of conscience. His life became joyless and purposeless. He kept silent about his sin and said of the result, 'My bones wasted away through my groaning all day long. For day and night your hand was heavy upon me; my strength was sapped as in the heat of summer' (Psalm 32:3, 4, NIV).

One day David decided to break the silence and come clean with God: 'Then I acknowledged my sin to you and did not cover up my iniquity. I said, "I will confess my transgressions to the Lord" – and you forgave the guilt of my sin' (Psalm 32:5, NIV). It was as if David was liberated from the darkness of a dungeon. The shackles of guilt fell off and the light of God's love shone into his heart again.

A husband who is cheating on his wife finds it difficult to look her in the eye and talk to her. He is uncomfortable in her presence. When we cheat on God, the One who loved us so much that He sent His only Son at the risk of eternal separation to be our Saviour, we find that we are not comfortable in His presence: we try to avoid Him. At such times we may give the impression that we are praying to Him but our heart is not in our prayer. 'These people honour me with their lips but their hearts are far from me' (Matthew 15:8, NIV). This statement can be made of many professed Christians today. God does not take account of prayers that merely come from the lips and not the heart. But when, like David, we pour out our hearts in confession to Him, the hostility between Him and us is removed; He showers us with forgiveness and takes delight in answering our prayers. We are friends once more.

In order for prayer to be acceptable to God, it must be coupled with a desire and a determination to confess and forsake all known sins.

Step 6: Pray from the heart

Some prayers sound more like entries in an oratorical contest than the opening of the heart to God. Someone defined prayer as the opening of the heart to God as to a friend. Many public prayers are designed to impress the audience of worshippers rather than to supplicate the throne of grace. Effective prayers are born of a soul-need and come from the heart. They come from hearts that are acutely conscious of their sinfulness.

Peter, one of Jesus' disciples, decided that he would follow his

Master's example by walking on water. The story is recorded in Matthew 14. Seeing Jesus walking on the sea one night Peter said, '. . . Tell me to come to you on the water.' 'Come,' said Jesus. Without any further prompting Peter stepped on the water and for a while was doing well. Apparently a strong wind arose and Peter lost his composure; he became afraid and began to sink. Scared and helpless, he cried out from the depths of his being, 'Lord, save me.' He had no time to think of long and complex sentences. It was a cry from the heart. God never turns away from the impassioned plea of His children as they recognize their own helplessness and look to Him.

At the prayer of Peter, Jesus reached out His hand and saved him. What a wonderful example of how God answers the prayers of those who call on Him in simple faith.

Step 7: Wait on the Lord

I used to be an ardent listener of 'Thought for Today' on BBC Radio 4. Rabbi Lionel Blue was my favourite presenter. He had the knack of making the complex simple by passing ideas through the filter of humour, stories and real-life experiences. Several years ago he told an apocryphal story about a man who had a passionate desire to meet God face to face. One morning the man was walking along the Sussex Downs when his dream came true: he met God face to face. The man was very excited. He told God he had been waiting a very long time to meet Him and that he had some questions to ask Him. God then told him to go on and ask his questions. The first question was, 'Is it true that a thousand years with You are like a minute?' 'Yes,' replied God. 'Is it true that a thousand pounds with You are like a penny?' 'Yes.' 'Can you give me one of those pennies?' 'Certainly; I will be happy to. Just wait a minute.'

If we want one of God's pennies, we may have to wait one of His minutes. He knows what is best for us. He will not be hurried into doing anything for us. However, when He rises up to act on our behalf, it is always at the right time. He always acts on time.

There are times when it appears that God is taking a long time to answer our prayers. At such times we must remember that He can see into the future where we cannot see. His eyes pierce the darkness where we are blind. He knows us more than we know ourselves. God knows our hurts, our pains and our loneliness. The Bible tells us that He knows our sorrows and records our tears. He knows the reason why tears fall from our eyes. He knows our thoughts, ways and words. A Book of Remembrance is written before Him for those who fear the Lord and think upon His name.

Wait on the Lord. 'Wait for the Lord; be strong and take heart and wait for the Lord' (Psalm 27:14). Our heavenly Father will not fail us.

Step 8: Accept God's answers

Often we do not know what to pray for. Our prayers are at times inward looking and self-centred. Romans 8:26, 27 indicates that when we pray, the Holy Spirit takes our prayers and presents them to God in an acceptable form: 'We do not know what we ought to pray for, but the Spirit himself intercedes for us with groans that words cannot express' (NIV).

God chooses to answer our prayers in ways that will prove a blessing to us. We must remember that He is not only concerned about satisfying our immediate needs; He is also leading us to our eternal home. He allows us to have experiences that shape our characters and prepare us for entrance into the earth made new. He is more concerned with long-term gains than with short-term benefits. This is a principle that I apply to the training of my own children. With long-term gains in mind God sometimes says 'Yes' to our requests, sometimes 'Wait' and other times 'No'.

Paul had a particular illness that seems to have been the cause of much discomfort. Tradition has it that it was a problem related to his eyesight. Whatever it was, he prayed to God most earnestly to take it away. His prayer was answered but the answer was 'No':

> To keep me from becoming conceited because of these surpassingly great revelations, there was given me a thorn in

my flesh, a messenger of Satan, to torment me. Three times I pleaded with the Lord to take it away from me. But he said to me, 'My grace is sufficient for you, for my power is made perfect in weakness.' (2 Corinthians 12:7-9, NIV)

When we trust God implicitly, we will accept His answers to our prayers as being in our best interest.

Step 9: Claim the promise of answered prayer

When David confessed his sins, as recorded in Psalm 32, he instantly accepted that his prayer was answered and that God had forgiven his sins. Faith grasps the reality of that which is not seen. Faith in God's promises is predicated upon his faithfulness. The New Testament is replete with texts that portray God as One who always fulfils His promises. For example, 1 John 1:9 says, 'If we confess our sins, He is faithful and just to forgive us our sins . . .' (KJV).

There are times when, after we have prayed, we feel no different emotionally than before we prayed. It is easy at such times to conclude that our prayer has not been heard. However, it is important to remember that God's acceptance of us is not based on our feelings but on His promises. Feelings are fickle and changeable but God's promises are sure, His love is unchanging. Prayer is not like a lottery, in which we most often lose but occasionally win. We can take God at His word and accept that every genuine prayer that is prayed in faith is answered. We win every time.

Step 10: Pray always

This was an injunction of the apostle Paul to the Christians in Thessalonica (1 Thessalonians 5:17). Many debates have taken place over the centuries as to the meaning of these words of the apostle. Those who have interpreted them to mean that the Christian is required to adopt a posture of prayer 24 hours a day have not made any provision for practical living. My understanding of the injunction is that Paul was urging his hearers to practise continuity in their prayer life. Prayer should not be spasmodic. There should be a constant spirit of prayer breathing through the Christian's life, even when engaged in the most mundane activities.

In addition to the spirit of prayer that pervades the life, Christians should also set aside time in their busy schedule to actively commune with God. The prophet Daniel had special times of prayer. He prayed three times each day. Jesus, our example, made prayer a priority in His life. Early in the morning He sought the face of His Father: 'Rising up a great while before day, He went out, and departed into a solitary place, and there prayed' (Mark 1:35, KJV). At the end of the day He also found time for active contact with His Father. 'Great multitudes came together to hear, and to be healed by Him of their infirmities. And He withdrew Himself into the wilderness and prayed' (Luke 5:15-16, KJV). Occasionally He prayed throughout the night: 'And it came to pass in those days, that He went out into a mountain to pray, and continued all night in prayer to God' (Luke 6:12, KJV).

'He [Jesus] was wholly dependent upon God, and in the secret place of prayer, He sought divine strength that He might go forth for duty and trial' (White, 1940, p. 363). If Jesus the Son of God felt a need to pray as much and as often as He did, how much more do we, poor and frail human beings, need to seek the face of our heavenly Father night and day, that He might strengthen us to live in this corrupt age?

Conclusion

Prayer is a privilege. Through prayer we enter the very throne-room of the King of the universe. Without appointment or courtly etiquette we enter His presence, knowing that He will listen and speak to each praying soul as if they were the only person in the universe.

God's power is available to those who seek it through prayer – power to heal, power to reconcile, power to live victorious Christian lives, power to witness. If Christians prayed more, this world would be a better place. The light of Truth would illuminate darkened minds and His grace would captivate the lives of many who aimlessly drift along.

Prayer is not an end in itself: it is merely the means to an end. The answers to prayer are the reasons for prayer.

> It is by answered prayers that human nature is enriched. The answered prayer brings us into constant and conscious communion with God, awakens and enlarges gratitude, and excites the melody and lofty inspiration of praise. Answered prayer is the mark of God in our praying. It is the exchange with heaven, and it establishes and realizes a relationship with the unseen. We give our prayers in exchange for the divine blessing. God accepts our prayers through the atoning blood and gives Himself, His presence, and His grace in return. (Bounds, 1977, p. 206)

References

Bounds, E. M. (1977) *The Best of E. M. Bounds on Prayer*, Grand Rapids, Michigan: Baker Book House.

Bounds, E. M. (1994) *The Essentials of Prayer*, Grand Rapids, Michigan: Baker Book House.

Morneau, Roger (1997) *The Incredible Power of Prayer*, Hagerstown, Maryland: Review and Herald Publishing Association.

White, Ellen G. (1940) *The Desire of Ages*, Mountain View, California: Pacific Press Publishing Association.

White, Ellen G. (1994) *The Ministry of Healing*, Grantham, Lincs: Stanborough Press.

HELP! I CAN'T PRAY

Delroy Hall

My name is Delroy Hall and I have been married to Paulette for eight years. We are the parents of two beautiful twin girls, Saffron and Jordan.

I was raised in a Christian home by parents who taught me the simplicity of godly living.

I became a Christian at the age of 20, and realized that God had called me for ministry at the age of 25. I spent the next four years resisting the call.

I have been a pastor since 1994 and have been in my current pastorate in Sheffield since 1996. It has excited and challenged me to the very core of my being.

My time in Sheffield has caused my attention to be focused on crucial issues of church growth, leadership training and development. Paulette often reminds me how fortunate I am because there are not many people who enjoy their work today. The future looks good and I am looking forward to getting there.

My wife is a continual source of inspiration and encouragement and I am learning to listen to her! Having a call into ministry at this hour, and being included in God's plan for the planet earth is an honour and a privilege for which I am grateful.

'Help! I can't pray.' How many times have those words been uttered, not just by new converts but by people who have been Christians for many years? Even for some seasoned Christians praying is no easy feat. What is it all about? Why should I pray? The questions are endless. The answers match the multiplicity of questions. I will attempt to suggest ways of developing the vital habit of prayer so that it becomes a delight and a pleasure, and not a tedious chore that seems to hinder the Christian journey.

Unfortunately, some Christians have explained prayer as a complex phenomenon. Definitions of prayer abound and often, after many explanations, some people are still none the wiser.

We are told, especially as new Christians, that we must pray. In the early days of my Christian life I did not think to ask questions of why and how I should pray. The main reason, I think, was due to the fact that I had been raised in a Christian home, and I learned prayer more by observation and absorption than by being made to sit down and be instructed in a didactic fashion.

Prayer, in my understanding of things, is simply building or developing a relationship with God. To the born-again believer God is not an 'out there' abstract object that has little or no interest in our lives. He wants to have a personal relationship with you and me. When I have been asked, 'How do you pray, or what is prayer?' I simply inform people that prayer is building a relationship with God. My next statement to the enquirer is in the form of a question, namely, how do you build a good relationship with someone? The response of those to whom I have posed such questions varies, but there are always common threads to people's answers. They consist chiefly of the individual spending time with someone, talking, communicating, i.e. suggesting a two-way process, not doing things to upset the other person, taking time to listen to the other individual, not doing all the talking (and if you do talk, giving the listener the opportunity to talk so that they can be listened to). In addition, the sharing or exchange of emotions is the real essence of relationships. These are just a few of the many ingredients that are necessary to establish good relationships.

For many individuals who have not had the privilege of being raised in a Christian home, the act of prayer might be difficult. However, it would be naïve of me to assume that people from non-church backgrounds do not and cannot pray. I have met many individuals who would not profess to have any particular affiliation to any church or religion, but religiously (and in some cases more so than professing Christians) read their Bibles and pray each night before they retire to bed.

The Bible is filled with dynamic prayers of men and women who were facing some form of personal or national crisis. Did their prayer lives begin on a high? I think not. They reached such levels of spirituality by a regular disciplined life of prayer, usually amidst times of great struggle. Let me illustrate one aspect of this growth in God. Our parents or Sunday School teacher informed most of us as children about the powerful event of Daniel in the den of lions (Daniel 6:1–24). At that stage of Daniel's life he was about 80 years old. Most of us, including myself, think of Daniel as being a young man. Where did he get his strength from to face such difficulty? Was this event his first test of faith? No, it was not. One of his first battles and tests of faith that is recorded is found when he was a young man, along with his friends Meshach, Shadrach and Abednego (Daniel 3). The story is that there was a command proclaimed by King Nebuchadnezzar, that at the sound of musical instruments all the inhabitants of Babylon would have to bow down and worship the king.

Daniel and his friends were faced with a dilemma: either to worship the king, or disobey his command, and suffer the consequences. They chose to disobey the king's decree. Their words were, 'If that is the case, our God whom we serve is able to deliver us from the burning fiery furnace, and he will deliver us from your hand, O king. But if not, let it be known to you, O king, that we do not serve your gods, nor will we worship the gold image that you have set up' (Daniel 3:17–18, NKJV). They were thrown into the fiery furnace, but survived. Much to the king's horror, he had thrown three people into the furnace, asked for it to be made hotter, then found the fourth person in the fire with the three, all alive and well.

Daniel developed spiritual staying power from a young age. In a similar fashion we develop the habit of prayer in small but manageable ways. One of the best starting points is a small booklet written by Robert D. Foster (n.d.). The idea has been used by the Navigators, a non-denominational Christian organization. Essentially, the author divides one's time allocated for prayer into four distinct categories. The acronym for this prayer pattern is ACTS. It is a similar pattern to that suggested by Jesus as he taught his disciples how to pray (Matthew 6). 'A' stands for adoration. This is the purest kind of prayer because it is all for God. Foster states quite rightly that 'you do not barge into the presence of God'. The 'C' stands for confession. Having seen

God, the author says, 'You want to be sure that you are cleansed of every sin.' 'T' is for thanksgiving. We are called to express our gratitude to God for all the things he has placed in our lives. One songwriter penned this song, 'Count Your Blessings'. The last line of the chorus says, 'and it will surprise you what the Lord has done'.

The last section of this time of prayer is 'S' for supplication. This is the part of prayer where we ask, or intercede, on behalf of other people, as well as ourselves. The seven minutes include a significant proportion for Bible reading. I would advocate this being given to all new converts, as it is very easily managed. The idea is that as you begin with something that is manageable you will be able to increase your time with the Saviour of your soul. Prayer for one hour a day is good, although it is not so much the amount of time spent, but it is more to do with the quality of the time spent, and the genuineness of our heart at the time of prayer.

There is an excellent scene in the gospels where Jesus walks on the water. The disciples think they have seen a ghost. Jesus assures them that they have not seen an illusion, but it really is him. To prove a point, Peter, one of Jesus' disciples, asks if he can walk on the water too. Jesus says to him, 'Come.' Peter steps out of the boat in obedience to the voice of Jesus. He finds himself walking on the water. Suddenly, the wind and water start to get boisterous. Peter begins to get anxious and fearful. He is distracted, and his focus is taken off Jesus. In his panic, he begins to sink. He does not have the time for a long, religious, theologically correct prayer, but he exclaims, 'Lord save me!' Jesus stretches out his hand and rescues Peter. Jesus rebukes Peter for his lack of faith. This 'arrow prayer' offered by Peter is short, sweet, to the point and comes from a genuine heart! (Matthew 14:22–33).

Prayer can take different forms. It can be short and pointed as described in the previous illustration. It can be silent as in the examples of the desert fathers who withdrew from society for extended times of prayer and reflection, and then would enter into cities to minister to people. Other forms of prayer are like those often spoken about by the likes of Thomas Merton, a

Carmelite monk who believed strongly in contemplative prayer. This type of prayer is one that is used for one's devotional life. Usually it is done silently and it is used more for the developing of the individual's private, intimate spiritual life with God.

There are the church prayers that are audible and can be heard throughout the congregation. Years ago, in some Pentecostal churches, and I dare say that the practice is still observed today by some, the audible prayer in a church setting is used as a sure sign of one being 'saved' and showing signs of spiritual growth.

Years ago when I was going through a particularly painful crisis I had the opportunity to talk with a very experienced and wise pastor. He said that he could not promise me, or any of his members anything, but one thing he could assure us of, was that, if we continued to pray, we would not backslide, or leave the Lord. I have valued those words ever since. Prayer is key to the progression of our spiritual life. Selwyn Hughes (1982, p. 9) seems to support the notion of the importance of developing a keen prayer life. It would seem that nowadays life has become so hectic that prayer for many is right at the bottom of the list of their daily priorities. In our pursuit of developing a prayer life our busy lifestyles make it increasingly difficult to slow down. We dart from one event to another and rarely, other than at the onset of a crisis, do we stand, stare and reflect about our life and the direction in which it is going.

As preachers, we can induce feelings of guilt and greater inadequacy in the life of Christians who regularly worship with us as we repeatedly tell them to pray when some are not even sure how to. A church member once told me that preachers keep telling people that they should be doing more of this or more of that, but fail to instruct their people how to do it. One of the beautiful things about prayer is that the more you do it and spend time cultivating a relationship with God, the more you will want to do it; but learning how to get started is usually the most difficult part.

Gordon MacDonald (1993, p. 70) states after presenting a lecture to a group of pastors that 'the world is full of disorganised people who have lost control of their time'. He continues by highlighting some of the areas that are symptomatic of the disorganized life. These are a few of them. He knows when there is a slipping into disorganization when the desk becomes cluttered, or when the interior of the car becomes strewn with rubbish. There are signs of disorganization when calls and appointments are missed. Disorganized Christians rarely enjoy intimacy with God; and finally, the quality of personal relationships usually reveals disorganization (1993, pp. 71–2). I personally would encourage readers to purchase a copy of the book written by MacDonald, as it is one of the modern Christian classics on the key elements necessary for establishing an enriching spiritual life in which prayer is key. MacDonald states quite boldly that 'time must be budgeted' (p. 73). So not being able to pray might have much to do with lack of time management rather than lack of techniques.

To develop a good relationship the conditions must be right. When you go to pray, attempt to find a suitable place: a place that is familiar and comfortable for you. It is helpful if you are able to find a special time to pray. It is true that you can pray anywhere and anytime, but having a special place in which to spend valuable time is better than praying on the run.

The previously mentioned booklet by the Navigators is a good and simple way into developing a prayer pattern.

Developing a prayer life takes time. Selwyn Hughes cites the fact that those who are experienced in praying need at least half an hour to achieve effectiveness (1982, p. 34). Isn't that true of human relationships? On initially meeting someone who we care about after a break, some of the introduction involves talking about the trivialities of the day or the time we have been absent from each other. It is only after the preliminaries are dealt with that the real conversation takes place.

Hughes further advocates that you must decide how long you are going to spend in prayer. You must decide what is adequate for you. Then, he suggests that you plan your time to cover the following three areas: looking at God, looking at yourself, and looking at others (p. 34).

In simple terms, looking at God means acknowledging ourselves as sinners and allowing the mercy of God to change our lives. He encourages us to invite his presence, but then we are not to run off, we are to 'linger' in his presence (p. 34). You will never be short in thanking God for all that he has done for you. Even the mere fact of being born in a land where we have easy access to sufficient food is something to thank him for.

The second aspect is praying for yourself and your own spiritual condition (p. 35). Hughes adds a note of explanation as some may say that your own needs should be considered last of all. He agrees in part, but he has discovered that if you pray over your own spiritual condition first, the purification that begins in you spills over into more effective prayers for others (pp. 35–6).

Looking at yourself is not about having the feelgood factor or ego massaging, but as we approach the mercy seat of grace in prayer we see our failings, weaknesses and sins. It is a time for confessing sins not yet repented of. The psalmist declares, 'if I regard sin in my heart the Lord will not hear me' (Psalm 66:18). This pouring out of our souls is not about self-abasement where we are left with a gross inferiority complex, but we are strengthened as we acknowledge who we are before God and how he delivers us from our burdens. If this prayer could be paraphrased in one simple sentence it might be, 'How can I be more like Jesus?'

We have confessed in the second section of the prayer and we are now left to intercede, or pray on behalf of others. Some people keep a list or a prayer book with individuals' names in it so they are reminded of whom and what to pray for. Praying for others means we must be specific. I have noticed that many times when people pray they are not specific in their requests. God certainly knows what we need, but he wants us to say it. In human terms we generally avoid making specific requests to people when we are unsure of the quality of our relationship with them. Uncertainty can also exist if we think that we do not deserve what we are asking for, or if we have a faulty image of God. There will also be difficulties if our heart does not truly desire what we are asking for. All this contributes to how effectively we pray. How you feel about yourself is a crucial aspect of prayer. When we go to pray we bring our entire self to the throne of God.

It is interesting to point out, and I have proved it from personal experience, that you might be going through life without an apparent care in the world. However, at the moment when you choose to pray it is as though all those things you have done wrong seem to confront you. You must deal with them before you can continue your heavenly discourse. The apostle Peter states an example of hindered prayers. He gives husbands a stiff rebuke in how they should treat their wives. He admonishes them that they are to treat their wives well so that 'their prayers will not be hindered' (1 Peter 3:7). This links in to Hughes' earlier suggestion of praying for ourselves first (1982, pp. 34–5).

One of the most important but neglected aspects of prayer is that after talking to God has ceased we ought to spend time waiting for God to respond to us. I was privileged to attend Spring Harvest in 1999. I was doubly privileged to hear Tony Campolo speak. One of the things that he said stuck forcibly in my mind, and that was, each day before he gets out of bed he spends approximately half an hour meditating on God. He begged us as Christians to spend more time listening to God and not continually demanding from him. I entirely endorse his statement, but I would add that, after a time of prayer and before we leave that sacred place and enter into the hustle and bustle of daily life, we spend time listening to him. Could it be that as we have spoken to God, he might want to say something to us? After all, we are in a relationship with him!

Another method of praying that I have found very effective is the use of a journal. This is not so much a diary, noting down appointments of the day, but rather a means of reflecting on that day's events. After recording the day's events through a process of reflecting on feelings, thoughts and meditation, the final thing is to write out a prayer. I initially felt uncomfortable with this method of prayer as I always thought prayers had to be verbal. Coming from the Pentecostal tradition, written prayers were not considered to be as authentic as verbal prayers. However, this type of prayer is for personal devotion and not for a public audience. Bill Hybels, in *Too Busy Not to Pray* (1996), observes the lives of famous people who had made their mark in society or in their chosen vocation and finds that most kept journals. The book that spoke to him in relation to keeping a journal was *Ordering Your Private World* by Gordon MacDonald. Keeping such a journal was something that he viewed with great scepticism: he was not that kind of reflective person. He was a 'get up and go' type of individual. So this method went against the grain. However, he tried it and, after much perseverance, he found it to be an invaluable part of his development as a leader.

Apart from praying or listening to God, the journal has a marvellous and invaluable feature of making one slow down the pace of life.

The method described by Hybels is to buy a spiral-bound pad. I personally use an A4 pad. At the top of the page you write, 'Yesterday' with the date and then write on that one page only. At the back of the journal a prayer is penned in response to what has been written, or anything that comes to mind. This prayer is then vocalized. This does not have to be prayed verbatim, but again, as you speak the prayer other things will come to mind. All this takes time but it is worth the effort. You may ask, if I write down the day's events is it not possible that it can become egocentric, and all I am doing is to overlook my faults? The journal as well as prayer depends on honesty. It is strange that as you write about the day's events you will begin to see into the depths of your own heart. Read the following insertion in MacDonald's journal. He was facing an enormous challenge in his ministry and while contemplating on it he penned these words:

> Lord, what do I really know about drawing upon your strength? I, with the shallow mind, the weak spirit, the minimal discipline. What is there of me that you could use? I have talents, but others have more and use them better. I have experience, but others have greater and have profited deeper. So what is there?
>
> Perhaps the answer lies somewhere in [Hudson] Taylor's comment: 'God uses men who are weak and feeble enough to lean on him.' But, Lord, I worry that while I may be weak

enough, will I be smart enough to know from whence comes my help?

Should you ordain that I do this task, what will sustain me? What of the sleepless nights when I shall be lonely? The seductions toward applause? The temptation to believe the symbols of leadership? What will keep my judgments clear, my mind sharp, my spirit filled? Now I ask honestly, am I able to receive this cup? What will convince me of the needs of the lost? What will keep me sensitive to the poor? What will make me listen? Pray? Study? Remain simple? O God, nothing but a visitation from thee. (1993, p. 145)

This is a lengthy passage, but it encapsulates the heart of one who is struggling inwardly to discern the will of God for his life. It is not a conflict with belief but a struggle for the right action. As you read this section you can almost feel the intense anguish that he is wrestling with. How many of us have had those experiences? They were not pleasant at the time, yet they were the fertile grounds of learning. How many of those experiences have we allowed to slip by without recording them? These writings are not for a once-only expression, but they are to be revisited to thank God for where he has brought us from. This struggle does not elevate the self, but it is the heart depending on the everlasting arms of Jesus.

Conclusion

There are many other techniques for praying that have not been mentioned here, but ultimately prayer is about spending time with God. He wants us to get to know him. For many years, writes Bill Hybels in his epigraph, 'I knew more about prayer than I had ever practised.' Does that sound familiar? Most of us feel a niggling guilt at not praying enough. Prayer takes time and stillness – and we're so *busy*! He found a way out and continues by saying, 'I did something absolutely radical, I prayed.'

Do not put off for tomorrow what you can start today. Begin to pray. Begin small and you will soon grow.

The individual who begins and continues to persevere in the act of prayer will find deep richness and experiences in God. As the apostle James encourages us, 'Do not merely listen to the word, and so deceive yourself. Do what it says' (James 1:22).

References

Foster, R. D. (n.d.) *Seven Minutes with God: How To Plan a Daily Quiet Time*, Colorado: Navipress.

Hughes, S. (1982) *Fifteen Ways to a More Effective Prayer Life*, Basingstoke: Marshalls Paperbacks.

MacDonald, G. (1993) *Ordering Your Private World: Setting Priorities*, Surrey: Highland Books.

Hybels, W. (1996) *Too Busy Not to Pray*, Leicester: Inter-Varsity Press.

PATIENCE IN PRAYER

Ron Brown

Revd R. O. Brown was born in Westmoreland, Jamaica and immigrated to the UK in 1959. He received the Lord Jesus Christ as his personal Saviour in July 1955 and eventually became a lay preacher and local church leader.

Revd Brown became a member of the New Testament Church of God in 1962 and served as District Youth Director. He was called to full-time ministry in 1963 when he became the pastor for the Gloucester NTCG, then Rugby, Walsall and served in Leicester as District Overseer.

He is married to Phyllis and they have two children, Melanie and Christopher, and one grandson, Kareem. In 1971 he was appointed Evangelism Director for the UK until he answered the call to the mission field in 1983. Revd Brown and his wife served as Missionary Overseers of the Church in Ghana from 1983 to 1992. On his return to the UK he was appointed pastor of his denomination's largest church in Brixton, London. He was appointed the National Overseer for the movement in 1994 and was awarded Doctor of Literature by the European Bible Seminary in 1995.

Revd Brown's motto is to know Christ better and to make him better known. One of his favourite scriptures is Philippians 3:10 (KJV): 'That I may know him and the power of his resurrection.'

It has been said that God answers all prayers, some with a 'Yes', some with a 'No', and some with a 'Wait'. The process of waiting will be given greater consideration as we develop this chapter.

It is sometimes hard to exercise patience, but do it we must, for in so doing we learn many lessons, receive many blessings and reap great rewards. Many of the treasures of this world – gold, silver, precious stones – are buried in mines deep in the heart of the earth. In order for us to get them and put them to useful purposes a process of mining has to be embarked upon. Likewise, in order to receive the blessings and the favour of God, the scriptural admonitions must be heeded. 'Wait upon the Lord, be of good courage and he shall strengthen your heart . . .' and 'in your patience possess your souls'.

In our present day, when almost everything can be had at a touch of a button – instant meals, instant remedies, instant solutions and quick fixes – it takes some discipline to be patient and to wait when the answer is delayed. The assurance which we have is that delay is not denial, and that through perseverance we shall receive. Again the scripture says everyone who continues to ask, receives, and they who seek, find; to those who continue to knock the doors will be opened. Jesus gave a parable in Luke 18:1–8 (NKJV):

> . . . that men always ought to pray and not lose heart, saying: 'There was in a certain city a judge who did not fear God nor regard man. Now there was a widow in that city; and she came to him, saying, "Get justice for me from my adversary".' And he would not for a while; but afterward he said within himself, 'Though I do not fear God nor regard man, yet because this widow troubles me I will avenge her, lest by her continual coming she weary me'. Then the Lord said, 'Hear what the unjust judge said. And shall God not avenge His own elect who cry out day and night to Him, though He bears long with them? I tell you that He will avenge them speedily'. Nevertheless, when the Son of Man comes, will He really find faith on the earth?

The sovereign move of God in answer to prayer cannot be hurried.

The model prayer in Matthew 6 demonstrates the picture of coming into the presence of the loving heavenly Father with thanksgiving to await his bidding and to see about his business. The prayer says, 'Hallowed be your name, your kingdom come, your will be done on earth as it is in heaven, for yours is the kingdom, yours is the power, yours is the glory.' This really is what prayer is about. It is not giving instructions to God, or even acquainting him with our needs and our wants, but rather waiting in his presence for his orders, to carry out his will, and in so doing, to positively affect his kingdom, give glory to his name and invite his blessings.

We shall now proceed to develop our subject from three aspects:

1. Patience in prayer through waiting.
2. Patience in prayer through watching.
3. Patience in prayer through worshipping.

Patience in prayer through waiting

Isaiah 40:31 (NKJV) says, 'But those who wait on the Lord shall renew their strength; they shall mount up with wings as eagles, they shall run, and not be weary, they shall walk, and not faint.' The strength derived from waiting on the Lord gives the power to live as victorious Christians to overcome temptation, to serve the Lord with gladness and to make a difference in our world. Waiting teaches us to rest with confidence in the presence of the Lord, to learn more about him and to be acquainted with his will and his ways. By this process the Holy Spirit accesses our lives, moulds us in the image of our Lord, and helps our development and growth.

To achieve any standard of excellence – in industry, in education or any walk of life – there must be hard work, patience and determination. If prayer, the greatest thing we can do, is to be effective, we must allow time, deliberation and patience.

W. D. Longfellow wrote:

> Take time to be holy, the world rushes on,
> Spend much time in secret with Jesus alone.
> By looking to Jesus, like Him thou shall be.
> Thy friends in thy conduct His likeness shall see.
>
> Take time to be holy, be calm in thy soul,
> Each thought and each temper beneath his control.
> Thus led by the Spirit to fountains of love,
> Thou soon shall be fitted for service above.

Our knowledge of the prayer-answering heavenly Father is that if we ask anything according to his will, he hears us; and because we know he hears us, we have by faith the petition that we ask for. There is no need then for anxiety, worry or frustration when waiting on the Lord. Though the answer tarries, it will come.

God sometimes tests our faith and endurance in order to prepare us for his blessings, and to perfect that which he has begun in us. Experience shows that when we receive gifts and benefits without realizing their true value, we sometimes misuse or even abuse them, but that for which we have input and have laboured, we learn to treasure. In the same way we would not put expensive jewellery or crystal in the hands of a toddler, or put a fast sports car in the hands of a young teenager; so God brings us to a place of development and maturity before he places certain blessings in our hands. Often, then, the waiting process prepares us to value the gifts and blessings that God gives in answer to prayer. It is to be noted that things that are common and easily obtained are less valued than those for which we have to mine deep in the heart of the earth.

C. H. Spurgeon has said: 'Let your fleece remain in the threshing floor of supplication till it is wet with the dew of heaven.' Because we know that God is unfailing and that he rewards those who diligently seek him, then it is joyful to patiently and prayerfully wait in his presence until the answer to prayer comes.

Moses waited 40 days in the presence of God and received the Commandments. Daniel waited 21 days and received answers to his questions with revelations concerning the coming of the Messiah and the end of the age. The disciples waited ten days, and Pentecost came. We would all be more effective in our ministry and receive more favour from the Lord if we learned to exercise patience in waiting upon God.

Our heavenly Father knows what things we have need of before we ask him. His eyes run throughout the earth to show his strength on behalf of those whose hearts are perfect towards him. He is able to do exceedingly abundantly above all we ask or think. We can be assured that asking according to his will, we have the petition that we asked for, when we ask in faith in the name of Jesus Christ. We find solace in the scriptural admonition:

> For you have need of patience so that after you have done the will of God you may receive the promise. For yet a little while and he who is coming will come and will not tarry. Now the just shall live by faith but if anyone draws back, my soul has no pleasure in him. (Hebrews 10: 36–38)

Patience in prayer through watching

Paul wrote to the Ephesians,

> Put on the whole armour of God that you may be able to stand against the wiles of the devil . . . praying always with all prayer and supplication in the Spirit, and watching thereunto with all perseverance and supplication for all saints; And for me, that utterance may be given unto me, that I may open my mouth boldly, to make known the mystery of the Gospel. (6:11–19, KJV)

Many of the lessons Jesus taught and the examples he demonstrated invite our watchfulness. The ten virgins fell asleep while waiting for the bridegroom. To the sleeping disciples he said, 'What? Could you not watch with me one hour? Watch and pray lest ye enter into temptation.' He would rise well before daybreak and go to a solitary place to pray. When his enemies wanted to betray and arrest him, they knew where to find him – in the garden of prayer.

When faced with the demon-possessed boy whom the disciples could not heal, Jesus said, 'However, this kind goeth not out but by prayer and fasting', signifying that only with much perseverance and watching, with fasting, can certain victories be won.

In the story of the man who came to his friend at midnight asking for three loaves, the friend was asleep with his children and did not wish to be disturbed; but because of the importunity, the determination, the perseverance of the friend outside, he got up and gave him as many loaves as he wanted.

If prayer is the central function of the new life of faith in Christ, it is obvious why our prayer life becomes the target against which Satan directs his fiery darts. We are told in scripture that it is by our watchfulness in prayer that we are able to quench the fiery darts that the wicked one constantly hurls at us. The enemy of our soul knows better than we do the effectiveness of watchfulness in prayer. If he can weaken our perseverance and distract our attention, he will succeed in piercing our armour, thus defeating us in the battles of life. He therefore fights our prayer life more than any other aspect of our Christian endeavour. The Bible warns us to look out and to watch for him, and to be prepared for the battles against principalities, powers and spiritual wickedness in high places. We should bear in mind that the carnal nature is enmity against God, and the flesh will not fight on the side of the spirit. If we refuse to wrestle, the enemy will still fight, but he will take our testimony. We cannot speak of being victorious until we have engaged the enemy; we cannot speak of overcoming until we have defeated the opponent.

Do you remember the times in your life of refreshing and revival, when the gifts and operations of the Spirit flowed freely with great anointing, when it was easy to rise early in the mornings and pray before you got involved with the day-to-day busy schedule? Why is it, then, that so often now we are most tired and sleepy when it is time to pray? Why is it that we find time to do so many other things, but often it's the times of prayer that have to be sacrificed to get other things done? In fact it is in the hour of temptation – when we need to pray most – that we are often distracted and robbed of the preciousness of victory through prayer.

The Bible tells us that the flesh wars against the spirit and the spirit against the flesh. It is so easy to talk much about prayer – many of our best sermons are geared to that subject – but the actual carrying out of the process is often neglected. Christians must not be ignorant of the enemy's devices, lest he gain an advantage over us.

Watching also speaks of taking careful guard of the stewardship that has been committed to our trust. Jude wrote to the early Church saying,

I exhort you to contend earnestly for the faith that was once delivered to the Saints. Building yourselves up in the most holy faith, praying always in the Holy Ghost and keeping yourselves in the love of God.

Philippians 2:12 tells us to work out our salvation with fear and trembling.

The story of Daniel's fasting and prayer reminds us how the powers of the prince of the air withheld the answer to Daniel's prayer. If Daniel had given up, the results would have been different. The angel said to Daniel, 'No one holds with me except Michael your prince . . .' (Daniel 10:21–11:1). Many of the battles in which we are engaged here on earth are also engaged in the heavens; our watchfulness in prayer on earth directly affects the outcome.

I recall the day when, on the mission field in Africa, I was taken ill, and for what seemed to be an hour or more was too weak to call for help from my secretary working next door to my office. Some time after, when visiting the UK, a young lady came to me and said, 'On such a date, at such a time, God commanded me to intercede on your behalf; I prayed for several hours before I could get any deliverance.' That was the exact moment when I was too weak to pray for myself or even to call for assistance, and God caused someone else to watch over me in prayer until my deliverance was secured.

The watchman in prayer therefore joins forces with God and with the angels to positively affect the work of God, not only in our personal life, but in the business of the kingdom on earth. Our role in prayer therefore is wider than that of our own home, church locality, or those we know and love. We are told in scripture to pray for kings, for those in authority. We therefore cannot be singular and selfish in our prayers, but should rather seek what is the mind and will of God and pray accordingly.

Our resolve, therefore, like that of Habakkuk, should be to 'stand up on my watch and set me upon the tower and will watch to see what he will say and what I shall answer when I am approved'.

Patience in prayer through worshipping

The very purpose for which we were created was for the pleasure and the glory of God.

Again, note the words of our Lord in Matthew 6: 'When you pray say our Father in heaven, hallowed be your name.' That means all honour, all praise, all glory be to your name. This must be our number one reason for praying. When we understand this, we will spend less time telling God what we want him to do, and how quickly we want him to do it. We will rather seize the opportunity to offer him the praise, thanksgiving and worship that is not only due to his name, but is also desired by him. Those who worship the Father must worship him in spirit and in truth, for the Father seeks such to worship him. How beautiful! How refreshing! How blessed when we come into his presence and know that we come because we love him, to give him that which is rightly his and to offer him tributes from a thankful heart. The fact about true worship is that when we selflessly offer to God that which is rightly his, he in turn pours out of his blessings upon us.

The Canaanite woman in Matthew 15 had followed Jesus for some time over the borders of Tyre and Sidon towards Galilee, crying, 'Have mercy on me son of David.' When she came to the place of understanding of Jesus' lordship, that he is the Son of God, and she worshipped him, the whole picture changed.

The first mention of worship in the Bible is in Genesis 22, where Abraham on Mount Moriah says to his servants, 'Tarry here with the ass while I and the lad go yonder and worship.' This worship called for a sacrifice, the sacrifice of his son; indeed, worship with all his heart, with all his soul, with all his mind and all his strength. It was at that place that he heard a voice from heaven, saying,

> By myself have I sworn said the Lord, because you have done this thing and have not withheld your son from me, that in blessing I will bless you, in multiplying I will multiply your descendants as the stars from heaven and as the sand that is upon the seashore and your descendants

shall possess the gates of their enemies. Indeed all nations of the earth shall be blessed because you have obeyed my voice.

The truth is that Abraham received more from God when he offered to him praise, worship and adoration, than when he made requests for things.

Isaiah saw the seraphim flying before the Lord and crying, 'Holy! Holy! Is the Lord of hosts' (Isaiah 6:3). Thousands of years later, John saw the heavenly creatures bowing before him and casting their crowns in worship and adoration before him (Revelation 4:10).

The greatest privilege of mankind therefore must be to be able to come into the presence of God and offer the sacrifices of worship and praise. Prayer gives us the opportunity to steal away from the cares and the hassle of a busy and hostile world, and to get alone with God in an intimate relationship in which we offer the honour and praise to him that is really his right. In this worshipful atmosphere the spirit of prayer will come to our aid and will help us, for he says, 'We know not how to pray as we ought. Likewise the spirit also helps our infirmities. But the Spirit himself makes intercession with groanings that cannot be uttered for he knows the mind of the Spirit' (Romans 8:26–27).

The beauty of worship is sometimes captured in the marriage service: 'With this ring I thee wed, with my body I thee worship.' The love shared and expressed there, is, according to Paul in Ephesians 5, but a small picture of the relationship between Christ and his Church. In this relationship we are able to fulfil what would be otherwise impossible – the biblical requirement to pray without ceasing. Wherever we are and in whatever situation, we can lift up our hands, we can lift our thoughts with a sigh, with a whisper, saying 'Father we love you, we worship and adore you.'

'I would that men pray everywhere, lifting up holy hands without wrath or doubting' is the wish of St Paul. The lifting of holy hands is in honour of him who is worthy of our praise. It is usually at this time that God reaches down his hand and touches us and makes us feel the very warm response of his love. 'There is a place of quietness near to the heart of God, a place where sin cannot molest near to the heart of God.' It is at this place we find the transforming power of God to mould us and make us into the image and likeness of his dear Son. In this atmosphere, the Holy Spirit's anointing comes and gives us an unction to minister in worship to God in prayer, sometimes in songs, in Hallelujahs, in joyful praise, in a sigh, a tear or in a heavenly language which is given to us through the baptism of the Holy Spirit: indeed, in groanings which cannot be uttered.

And not only so, but we glory in tribulations, knowing that tribulations produce patience, and patience character, and character hope.

Lord teach us to pray, teach us to wait, teach us to worship, teach us to watch.

PRAYING FOR A PARTNER

Pall Singh

Pall Singh is from a Sikh background and experienced having to leave home when he became a Christian. He trained at Birmingham Bible Institute from 1974 to 1977 and has worked with Solihull Christian Fellowship for 21 years. During this period he has been manager of a Christian bookshop, then later a youth/schools worker and an elder. Pall married Joy in 1983 and they have two children, Josiah and Jasmine. He is now the Director of East + West Ministry, which is working in the British Asian community, by providing a safe house for Asian women. He is the team leader with a pioneering weekly gathering, 'Sanctuary', which presents Christ to British Asians in culturally relevant ways. The Trust offers training through 'Asian Equip' to individuals, churches and Christian organizations nationally.

Therefore, I urge you, brothers, in view of God's mercy, to offer your bodies as living sacrifices, holy and pleasing to God – this is your spiritual act of worship. Do not conform any longer to the pattern of this world, but be transformed by the renewing of your mind. Then you will be able to test and approve what God's will is – his good, pleasing and perfect will. (Romans 12:1–2, NIV)

God's will for your life is good, pleasing and perfect; in prayer we are asking for his will to be released in our lives. First, we need to come to a place of sacrifice and abandonment to God and his purposes for our lives, but there is always a price to pay. For some this may mean making some radical changes, refusing to live at the level of compromise. Many Christians struggle so hard to find a fellow Christian who is compatible to them, that they settle for second best, marrying an unbeliever out of desperation that they will not find *the* one – only to discover later it was a serious mistake that often ends in tears.

God wants the best for your life: from the beginning he said, 'It is not good for the man to be alone. I will make a helper suitable for him' (Genesis 2:18, NIV).

Sharing your life in loving union with another is normal and natural and God-intended. He has created us in his image with an essential need at our very core for closeness, friendship, love and intimacy. A marriage partner is the natural relationship where we look to find an answer to our deep needs; however, not all our needs can be met in one person. Friends of our own gender fulfil a different role, as do relationships with others from the opposite sex. We should not look to our partner to meet every need we have; this is impossible for one person to do and leads to disillusionment later. In prayer we are rightly putting our future firmly in God's strong hands and learning to trust him daily. You may find compatibility with a number of 'good friends' of the opposite sex, but only through prayer will God reveal the right companion; the wrong decision can bring grief and pain to those concerned. When we are seeking God's best in this matter we must leave space for him to work supernaturally. His timetable is always perfect, so don't jump ahead of him; you may be tempted by pressure or pleasure and miss the best. It can be very frustrating to continually hear God saying 'Wait', but it is worth it. We live in age where it's 'Buy now pay later', why wait? Personally, I waited until I was 28 years old before the Lord brought Joy, now my wife, into my life – she was worth the wait! God never disappoints. Many times, like Abram, I was tempted to become impatient and listen to other voices and take short cuts, but I was kept by the power of God and the prayers of the saints.

Arrange that marriage

I come from a Sikh background where traditionally it's the responsibility of the 'family' to arrange the wedding. This long process is often done with thoughtful consideration for all the parties involved. However, sometimes it is not, with the families only looking to their standing in the community, their 'izzat', and not the happiness or otherwise of the child. I am not against 'arranged marriages' when they are performed with the full consent of the young people concerned, but I strongly disagree when these arrangements are forced on people against their will, as happened in my case. My family wanted to marry me to someone from India, who I had never met. Because of my faith in Christ, I was unwilling to marry an unbeliever and compromise my faith. This eventually meant leaving home in order to make a stand to my family that I was serious about putting God first in my life and that I trusted him to find me a partner. It was not easy to wait – it was ten years before I married. I had to endure their looks, gossip and comments, and it was painful to see their 'izzat' in the community go down because of me. The British Asian community is slowly moving towards the idea that they can assist their children in finding a partner without necessarily arranging it.

Perhaps Western Christians have placed the responsibility of marriage too heavily on the shoulders of the individual, without seeing the need to assist the single people in their churches. The Church needs to understand how to be true family to each other without taking away God's gift of free will. We will certainly need to help new Asian believers find their future partners, as for most, the concept of 'dating' or 'going out' is culturally alien; for them, love begins after marriage. We can learn a lot from each other if we look as a church for new ways of courting, taking the best from all cultures. This is particularly relevant in the youth groups, where the pairing off and heavy petting with different people every other week needs challenging, especially if groups are going to be able to reach out to the Asian young people. Our young people need encouraging to have healthy friendships with each other and be an alternative to the culture of the 'world' which considers you not to be worth anything unless you are a pair, however short-lived that pairing may be. They are under so much pressure, and they really do need our open, frank and honest support.

Mr/Miss Right

Don't waste your time looking for the person you think will be Mr/Miss Right – our eyes can deceive us. Instead, work on the development of your character; your greatest feature of attraction isn't your body but your personality and character. 'Choose a wife rather by your ear than your eye' (Thomas Fuller).

Pray, trusting God to bring the right man or woman into your life and prepare now for the future by learning to build friendships that are based on love and appreciation. We need to discover that one person in the future will not fulfil all our needs, but God has designed us for a network of relationships in his kingdom. The sexual bond in marriage is exclusive between two people, but friendship with others should be inclusive. In praying for your partner, seek wise counsel and prayer support from others you respect, and be prepared to share your heart and feelings in open fellowship.

Among many who prayed for me, one godly person stands out – Henry Brash Bonsall, the founder of Birmingham Bible Institute, who was Principal during my years as a student from 1974 to 1977. From our initial meeting to the final valedictory service, he would always pray for my future partner, and the Lord answered his prayer! Make sure another man or woman of God is praying for you today; many times the prayers of children, new believers and older people can be powerful. God can use Christians and not-yet Christians to answer your prayers by introducing you to someone who will be your future partner. Pray that the Holy Spirit will be actively preparing both of you.

Life doesn't begin with marriage but with God; therefore, deepen your love for him. Pray for someone who loves Jesus with all their heart, mind, will and soul. Seek spiritual compatibility and put God first in the relationship without compromising your faith, and the Lord will honour your stand.

Two wrongs don't make a Mr Right

Many have fallen into the trap of thinking that God wants them to marry someone unsaved and that through their witness the person will become a Christian. In some cases this has happened, but in most it has been disastrous, and it is often God who gets the blame! Recently, a Christian friend thought there was little 'talent' in the church and sought for a girlfriend in the world. After a short engagement, and two months into their marriage, he realized what a big mistake he had made and a few months later they were divorced. God's will is so clear in scripture: 'Do not be yoked together with unbelievers' (2 Corinthians 6:14, NIV).

The reason why God doesn't want you to wed someone unsaved is because he wants you to share and communicate with each other on all levels – physically, mentally, emotionally and spiritually. The praying must continue into the marriage; as you pray together you will grow together in Christ.

My attraction to Joy was beyond the physical, and beyond her wild hair styles to her sensitivity to God! When we first met, she wasn't even a Christian, but God was at work in her life and I waited and prayed. Three years later she turned up at church, much to my surprise and joy.

My good friend Gerald Coates says, 'God is doing more things behind our backs than in front of our faces.' God may be answering your prayers right now, behind your back, and one day they will become a reality.

Stop waiting

Start praying, then leave things in God's hands; stop daydreaming, putting your life on hold, and enjoy life to the full now! To make friends, you must show yourself to be friendly and see the grace of God at work in others. God's plan for your life includes today, and our future doesn't depend on our past but on God. Be yourself with God and learn to give yourself in service to others; there are opportunities for you to work for God in this nation and overseas. Take the opportunity to do things now that will have limitations one day, with responsibilities of family life.

Be honest with God

The following is a heartfelt letter from my dear friend Janie, who has been single over a period of time:

> I believe praying for a partner can almost become an obsession. I know I began to look at every fellow wondering if he was 'the one' and often as a result, failed to enjoy whatever was going on around me. It's almost as if singles need to be helped to continue enjoying ordinary activities while 'waiting'. I believe that having scriptures quoted, like 'God will be your husband' and 'Jesus will meet all your needs', at certain times of waiting for Mr Right to come along, is NOT a blessing, or of particular help. In a way it's reinforcing your deepest fear, namely that Mr Right just may not come along. Another area is when the fellow you're going with turns out not to be the one. You pray to do the right thing and feel God say, 'Give him up, give him back to me.' You do it believing somewhere, deep down inside that God, being the gracious one he is, will give him back to you. You are *sure* in your heart, way at the back God is only testing you and if you do and say the right things all will be well. I *did* give you everything Lord and you took it. You meant every word you said, didn't you? 'Yes, I did' God said. It then knocks you sideways to find that God actually means what he says and that you are not going to get the person back in the end. Devastating! How can God get it so wrong. I know he is Mr Right so why can't the Lord? I used to ask the Lord to remove all emotions from me as the pain of waiting (and no bus coming along . . .) was too great to bear. It took counselling from a pastor to learn that this type

of desire and prayer was wrong, particularly when my heart's desire was that this emotion should, in fact, be put into operation.

God feels our painful emotions, disappointments, and, as his children, he is committed to our present and future destiny, for his perfect will to be accomplished in our lives.

Keep fit

> But you, dear friends, build yourselves up in your most holy faith and pray in the Holy Spirit. Keep yourselves in God's love as you wait . . . (Jude 20, 21, NIV)

As we wait, God encourages us to keep building ourselves up in faith, but often Satan, the enemy, will discourage us and put us under condemnation because our prayers don't seem answered yet. Remember, only God knows what is going to happen in the future. We are called to live by faith, not by sight; we must keep trusting God every day and believing that we will receive more strength to perform his will.

Keep on praying

'. . . pray in the Holy Spirit'. Every Christian has the Holy Spirit at the point of their spiritual birth, but many times in our Christian experience we need to be filled with the power of the Holy Spirit. It is the person of the Spirit that helps us to pray in tune with God's will, and at times prays through us to the heavenly Father. Pray in tongues as the Spirit leads you and pray in your mother tongue as your mind leads. Prayer is a spiritual activity that needs to be inspired by God's Spirit and word. Build yourself up today by praying in the Spirit and don't give up! Build yourself a good network of people who can hold you up when you feel weary or weak. It is good to have a pre-arranged mechanism like a prayer chain or one special prayer friend with whom you can be totally honest: someone who you can admit your weaknesses to without feeling ashamed.

Keep yourself in God's love

'Keep yourselves in God's love as you wait . . .' (Jude 21, NIV). God's unconditional love never stops flowing towards us, but we must keep ourselves in that flow, day by day. Receive from the Lord every day his incredible love that accepts, forgives and heals our hurts. The partner you are praying for can never replace his love, only supplement it; this divine love is from God alone.

Jesus was single

In the Bible God makes it clear that he is for marriage and also says 'Yes' to singleness for the purpose of full dedication to his work. Our Western culture and sometimes the Church can dictate that singleness is second class and that something is wrong with you. The apostle Paul wrote:

> Sometimes I wish everyone were single like me – a simpler life in many ways! But celibacy is not for everyone any more than marriage is. God gives the gift of single life to some, the gift of the married life to others. I do, though, tell the unmarried and widows that singleness might well be the best thing for them, as it has been for me (1 Corinthians 7:7–8). (Peterson, 1993)

It is clear that wedding bells are not for everyone and that singleness can sometimes be better than marriage. It's a myth to believe that every Christian will get married, and assume that they will miss out in life without a partner. You are not a failure, a loser, a misfit or abnormal, because you belong to the category of singleness; never allow yourself or others to put you under condemnation. Go for it! Live life to the full, God is for you! Jesus was single too.

References

Hansel, T. (1987) *Holy Sweat*, Word.

Peterson, Eugene H. (1993) *The Message*, Navpress.

A PRAYERFUL LIFE

Hughes Redhead

Hughes Redhead was born on 21 September 1952 in Grenada in the Caribbean, and arrived in England at the age of nine. He is married to Patricia and has three children: Luke, Marcus and Rebecca.

Hughes was baptized at fifteen, and baptized with the Holy Spirit about a year later. He served in various ministries at the local church in which he grew up. He also served as a regional youth leader and as a regional and national evangelist.

Hughes is currently Senior Minister of The Hope of Rotherham Church. He has been speaking prophetically into Rotherham for the past seven years. The Church, he believes, must engage the community.

'I can't pray,' wailed Bob.
'Then don't,' I said; 'Just talk to God.'
Bob was the latest in a line of people I had tried to help in their struggle with prayer: struggles ranging from guilt that they were not praying enough or not praying the right prayer due to uncertainty about whether God would give them an answer. Some Christians have never known a time, since coming to faith in Jesus, when they did not have difficulty with the issue of prayer.

Getting over the prayer meeting hurdle

I can still remember the church in which I grew up, a Black Pentecostal church. When it came to prayer you had to be ready when called at a moment's notice. 'Brother Redhead will pray': but I didn't hear. I was fifteen and someone or something had distracted me. An elbow in my ribs from a good friend looking out for me brought me back to my senses and to where I was standing. It was the Sunday night service and a hundred pairs of eyes were tightly shut and waiting for me to lead in prayer. The pastor had his left eye closed and his right wide open, rolling, looking in my direction. I was thinking, as I looked at the eye, that only lizards could do that. Then it was too late. 'Sister M. Johnson will pray' instructed the pastor. 'Thank you Jesus,' Mavis Johnson began, and with encouragements of 'Amens' and 'Praise the Lord' around the room Sister Mavis in no time broke through any barriers I might have erected to the blessings. After my hesitation she was chosen because she was a sure bet. I, on the other hand, had to put up with looks which asked 'What have you been up to that you could not pray?' In the end no one made a big deal of it. As one person reminded himself, 'There but for the grace of God go I.'

Twenty-three years later I was sitting in a house group of a charismatic church: a new experience for me. Everyone was making every effort to avoid being 'heavy'. It didn't take me very long to twig that my style of praying fell into the 'heavy' category. All the other prayers were short, well structured and definitely light. How do people get to say prayers in such a clear, neat-and-tidy way, I wondered. Possibly to recover from a heaviness I had injected into the meeting, everyone was encouraged to relax and tell a joke. I passed on my turn; I didn't know many jokes, certainly none for church services. One brother appeared to have a ministry in telling them. Finally it was the turn of a young man who was, by all account, taking the smallest, almost imperceptible steps towards commitment to Christ. His joke – erotica – left everyone looking for somewhere to hide. Within weeks I felt settled in this more relaxed mode of small-group meetings, but with some reservations. Then out of the blue, one Sunday morning there was teaching on prayer and its importance. In the following weeks we were directed to attend serious prayer meetings, have quiet times and purchase books and audio tapes on prayer. I was even offered ministry to help me strengthen my prayer life.

Now that I am leading a local church, my own experiences help me to have an empathy with our people who struggle with prayer. A few years ago, to assist me in dealing with the difficulties many had with praying aloud in our prayer meetings, I decided to enlist the help of Teresa, our number one prayer warrior. Teresa appeared to take literally the scripture 'pray without ceasing'. 'I need you to help me with the people who struggle in prayer,' I said one day. I was driving, and Teresa was in the front passenger seat. I had to concentrate on the road, but out of the corner of my left eye I could see Teresa shuffling as she struggled with my request. 'Hughes, the people don't want to pray.' She said it in a tone which showed concern that I did not discern the obvious. 'Well, the fact that they come to the prayer meeting every week suggests that they do want to pray but have real difficulty in praying aloud.' I was determined that we found solutions, which we could all have ownership of. 'Maybe it's the structure of our meetings,' I added. 'We could sometimes split up into smaller groups which would be less intimidating.'

Teresa had given me enough time to have my say, and was dying to answer. 'But if people have a relationship with God and are used to praying at home, surely they can pray anywhere?' 'Yes,' I said, 'they can pray anywhere but not necessarily pray out aloud. It may even be that some are intimidated by those of us who are confident and at home with the cut-and-thrust of our prayer meetings.' 'But who are we praying to, Hughes – 'God or man?' Sister T was a true warrior, but this was too great a leap for her. The impasse was a clash of cultures.

After my discussion with Teresa I decided that I needed to lead the way and have everyone follow. I had group discussions and interviewed a number of individuals for their views on prayer. Then I started an experiment. First, everyone was made to understand that praying silently was one option. Our new-style prayer meetings commenced with short breakthrough prayers by those who were most confident. They were followed by the people who, for a variety of reasons, were uncomfortable with praying out in a group. We would call out the names of those who felt they needed their space to pray without the danger of starting the same time as another person and the ensuing embarrassment they would feel. For others who would run a mile if their name were called to pray, longer pauses were left between prayers for them to join in without them feeling that they were trying to hop onto a moving bus. One interviewee had said to me, 'I'm not going to fight to get the chance to pray.' And to satisfy the other end of the prayer spectrum we called for 'concerts of prayer', where everyone would pray at the same time. Splitting up into smaller groups was also used to good effect.

The result was a release of more people to pray freely and effectively. But the most important input into this whole process was not planned. As people developed stronger relationships in an atmosphere of love and trust it was easier to be relaxed about what different people brought to the prayer: a song, a reading, a powerful dynamic prayer, a short, barely audible prayer of thanksgiving, a prophecy, a word of encouragement and, dare I say it, even something amusing.

Conversations with God

All this, however, is a world away from what I would call a prayerful life. It is not about attending prayer meetings. It is not a life of prayer which smacks of living to eat instead of eating to live. It's as I had said to Bob, 'Stop trying to pray and start talking to God.' I know that prayer can range from thanksgiving and praise, through supplication and intercessions right on to spiritual warfare. However, my definition of a prayerful life is one of walking and talking with God, of conversations with our heavenly Father.

Adam and Eve

I can imagine that the best parts of life for Adam and Eve in the Garden of Eden were the times they spent with God, walking and talking with him in the 'cool of the day'. They must have had some great conversations. What did God tell them about the sun, the moon, the planets in our solar system, about our galaxy and other galaxies? Approaching him was not to them something heavy or tortuous but simply communing and conversing with their Father and Friend. When they asked him a question he gave an answer. I see them being glad to see him approaching as they took every opportunity to be close to him, knowing that they and everything around them were made, loved and sustained by him.

Enoch

We know very little about Enoch, the son of Jared and father of Methuselah. In the New Testament writings Jude quotes a prophecy from him. Apart from that, the only thing we are told is that he walked with God and that at the age of 365 years God took him from the earth. He had spent over 300 years walking and talking with God; three centuries of conversations with his Creator, with his Friend. Then, as if to overcome the limitations to their fellowship which a world populated by the rebellious imposed, Enoch sacrificed a further 600 years on earth to be closer to God. His was a prayerful life.

Abraham

What I believe to be one of the greatest prayers of intercession was spoken as a conversation between two people – Abraham and one of three visitors who came to his camp:

> Then the LORD said, 'The outcry against Sodom and Gomorrah is so great and their sin so grievous that I will go down and see if what they have done is as bad as the outcry that has reached me. If not, I will know.' The men turned away and went toward Sodom, but Abraham remained standing before the LORD. Then Abraham approached him and said: 'Will you sweep away the righteous with the wicked? What if there are fifty righteous people in the city? Will you really sweep it away and not spare the place for the sake of fifty righteous people in it? Far be it from you to do such a thing – to kill the righteous with the wicked; treating the righteous and the wicked alike. Far be it from you! Will not the Judge of all the earth do right?' The LORD said, 'If I find fifty righteous people in the city of Sodom, I will spare the whole place for their sake.' Then Abraham spoke up again: 'Now that I have been so bold as to speak to the Lord, though I am nothing but dust and ashes, what if the number of the righteous is five less than fifty? Will you destroy the whole city because of five people?' 'If I find forty-five there,'

he said, 'I will not destroy it.' Once again he spoke to him, 'What if only forty are found there?' He said, 'For the sake of forty, I will not do it'. (Genesis 18:20–29, NIV)

Abraham continued to ask for a reduction in the number of people needed to be found in Sodom to save it from destruction. God finally agreed not to destroy Sodom if there were as few as ten righteous people found. Something as serious as the saving of a number of cities was not conducted in an atmosphere which suggested that Abraham had to wrestle a response out of God with blood, sweat and tears, although I recognize that there is a place for all three. Neither was there any suggestion that what God agreed to was done grudgingly.

Samuel

It is Moses who in the Bible is shown more than any other person in conversation with God. But it is the life of the prophet Samuel which, for me, serves as a model for walking and talking with God which people today can relate to, especially if one adds the use of the gifts of prophecy and words of knowledge. Samuel was conceived in answer to his mother's prayer. Then, as a small child, God called his name, and we see the start of what become a close relationship between him and God:

> Then God called Samuel. Samuel answered, 'Here I am.' And he ran to Eli and said, 'Here I am; you called me.' But Eli said, 'I did not call; go back and lie down.' So he went and lay down. Again the Lord called, 'Samuel!' And Samuel got up and went to Eli and said, 'Here I am; you called me.' 'My son,' Eli said, 'I did not call; go back and lie down.' Now Samuel did not yet know the LORD: The word of the LORD had not yet been revealed to him. (1 Samuel 3:4–7, NIV)

Finally Eli realized that it was God calling Samuel and guided him in responding to God: 'Then the LORD came and stood there, calling as at the other times, "Samuel! Samuel!" Then

Samuel said, "Speak, for your servant is listening"' (1 Samuel 3:10, NIV).

As Samuel grew, he continued to listen to and hear from God. Then as an old man, after years of walking and talking with God, he was sent to Bethlehem to anoint a new king following Saul's rebellion. As each one of the sons of Jesse was presented to him he asked God whether that one was to be the next king of Israel, but not before he made the mistake of trying to guess the answer:

> When they arrived, Samuel saw Eliab and thought, 'Surely the LORD's anointed stands here before the LORD.' But the LORD said to Samuel, 'Do not consider his appearance or his height, for I have rejected him. The LORD does not look at the things man looks at. Man looks at the outward appearance, but the LORD looks at the heart'. (1 Samuel 16: 6–7, NIV)

And a right heart-attitude is essential for conversation with God. In a prayer meeting, or other church meeting, what we say takes account of the people listening, and unfortunately our prayers can be directed more to those people than to God to whom it is addressed. But when we are in conversation with God, he tells us what he thinks about the things we are saying to him.

A personal testimony

I would not want to guess at the sort of life I would be living if God did not tell me what he thought about the things I was saying to him. I'm not sure that our fellowship would have got very far if he gave no answers to my questions, or indeed if I failed to respond to him. By the age of seven I was very aware that I was not alone and that God was with me. That knowledge and awareness of God was both a source of great comfort and great difficulties. When I was about six I had a recurring nightmare in which my way would suddenly be barred by someone frightening and evil. However fast I ran, when I stopped, they would be there to confront me. Finally I told my mum. Her response was, 'Don't be afraid if they were to kill you; the Lord will resurrect you.' That night I had the same dream and stood my ground. I was killed. I could see myself lying on the ground. Suddenly I stood on my feet, resurrected, not even afraid of death. I never had that dream again. I also learned to go to God about my difficulties rather than going to my mum. But my relationship with God made my teenage years sheer torment. I didn't want to share all my experiences with him. I reasoned that I was justified in not praying about things like exams because it was unfair to the other children. Unfortunately it also meant that there was no need for me to give thanks to him for help and support.

When I had to fight at school I would sometimes apologise to God in advance but point out that there was no other way. I did agree that I would not be the one to start a fight and I would not hurt anyone so badly that it would get in the papers and cause people to reject the Gospel when, in the future, I came to preach it. It was at times like these that I did not expect an answer and did not wait for one. But even there, in my crazy, mixed-up teenage world, God showed me that he was with me. When I was fifteen, a school prefect, and in the fourth year at secondary school (now known as Year Ten), the pupils who chose to leave at the end of the fourth year decided to beat me up on the last day of term. As a prefect I had given them a hard time. They also decided that they needed the support of leavers from a neighbouring school. I knew that I could not fight them all so I decided to take my scout's knife to school for protection. However, my dad confiscated the knife when my sister informed him of my plans. I hadn't spoken to God about it because that simply complicated matters.

On the last day of term the leavers smashed up the toilets before leaving early. At 3.30 that afternoon, as I walked down the long drive from the school to the main road, I accepted that I would have to take a beating but I also mapped out the parts of the body and the damage I would inflict on the first and possibly the second of my attackers. As I neared the end of the drive, there, directly before me at the side of the main road, stood a burley policeman in front of his panda car. There was no time for me to work out how such a big man could fit into such a small car because, from my right, moving along the main road were the school-leavers from the two schools. We met at the end of the drive. But seeing the policeman, they kept on going, past the drive and up the road; I turned right and walked home in the direction they had come. The policeman stood and watched. There, at the age of fifteen, I knew that the presence of that police officer at the school gate was the work of God and that I had to learn to include him in every area of my life.

I have not been as successful as I would have liked in putting that lesson into practice, but fifteen years after the incident at the school I was much more willing to share my thoughts with God and listen to what he had to say to me. I can't remember where I was, but the Spirit told me that there were 30 people in our church who were not baptized with the Spirit and that I should go and pray for them to receive the Spirit. I wasn't aware that there were so many, so I decided to make a list. I recorded 28 names. Since the Holy Spirit couldn't get it wrong and I knew I'd heard correctly, I decided that either two people who were not filled with the Spirit were hiding, or that they believed they had received the Spirit when they had not. Most of the 28 were made up of people who, over the years, failed to receive the Spirit when others, including newcomers, were blessed with the gift. They were the hard cases who had sweated too long and too hard at too many 'altar calls'. Over the following three weeks I met with, talked to and prayed with most of them. This resulted in at least seventeen of them receiving the Spirit. They ranged from a young man I had led to Christ the week before, baptizing him in water two hours after he had made a confession of faith, to one brother who had been a Christian for 21 years. I knew that the brother loved singing, so after praying for him and seeing him filled and speaking in a new language, I asked whether he wanted to sing with the Spirit. He said yes, so I prayed for him again and he began to sing, with chorus and verses. It was all so easy, yet in the past we had tried so hard; we had prayed so hard.

One memorable day during those three weeks I joined my mum in praying with a couple and their adult daughter. Their neighbour, a young woman, was visiting and joined the prayer. The couple and the neighbour received the Spirit. From there I went to visit another couple. They were expecting me because the husband, who had come to faith in Christ fifteen years previously and been very involved in the church, had not yet received the Spirit. I spoke to him, prayed for him and he received the Spirit. 'Do you want to sing with the Spirit?' I asked. He did, so I laid my hands on him and prayed. Then I heard his wife singing with the Spirit. 'Haven't you sung in the Spirit before?' I asked. 'No,' she replied, 'but I always wanted to.'

It's so much easier when we hear God and follow his instructions. Some years previously, when I was the church youth leader, I visited a young man and led him and his two friends with him to pray and ask Jesus to come into their lives. They did, and I was overjoyed. Just as I was walking to the front door to leave, the Spirit said to me, 'That was too easy – go back and make it more difficult.' I'd never heard anything like that before; three new people just entered the kingdom of God and I was being asked to risk them rejecting Christ. But I was in no doubt that the Holy Spirit had spoken to me, so I went back and put as much effort into making it difficult for them to continue with their decision as I did to get the decision in the first place. I told them that following Jesus meant that they belonged to him, that he would be their Lord and King and that whatever he said they would have to do, wherever he sent them they would have to go. I then asked them for the second time if they were willing to follow Jesus. Each one said 'No'. When I asked why they had changed their minds, the leader of the group said that Jesus expected too much. That day the Spirit taught me the danger of simply presenting Jesus only as Saviour and not also as Lord and King. Without the help of the Spirit I could have been responsible for slipping into peddling cheap grace, where people believe that they can come to faith without obedience – that they can become a Christian without following Jesus.

In walking and talking with God – more specifically, in conversations with the Holy Spirit – we can share with him what is on our hearts, our hopes and fears, and hear from him the words by which we can and must live.

BECOMING A HANDMAID OF THE LORD

Elizabeth Murove

Elizabeth Murove is the founder of Triumph International. She had been involved in the ministry of intercession for the previous seven years after which God called her to be 'A voice crying out in the wilderness.' She has a prophetic command for Africa to Triumph! She has been proclaiming this message from Zimbabwe (her home country) and is now extending this to the rest of Africa. She has a powerful ministry of teaching prayer and intercession for the healing of the nations. In Zimbabwe she has planted prayer cells in 21 cities and the number is multiplying weekly.

Elizabeth is a widow with four children. In the past she has pioneered outreach work to the homeless in London. She has compassion for widows and the fatherless; this has seen her pleading and agonizing before the Lord for their well-being. She wants to see the Church of Jesus Christ rise up to take responsibility for these families. Even now the church in Zimbabwe is being challenged to answer this call.

I moved into south London in 1991, to be near King's College Hospital where I was training to become a midwife. While my husband and children were in Africa, I spent most of my spare time reading the Bible and praying for them. Eventually I had to move out of hospital accommodation and look for a bigger place in which to live, and moved to Peckham where I soon joined a local church. The teaching there was sound and I grew quickly in the Lord. I made friends with a girl there who also loved to pray and we would meet two or three times a week to pray for our church. Sometimes we would fast 21 days for the leadership or for the different church ministries. It was amazing how, on some Sundays, we would hear our pastor preach on issues that God had been speaking to us about during our prayer time. At this time my spiritual ears became really tuned to hear the voice of God, I also started to see visions on regular occasions and learned to interpret them and to discern what the Holy Spirit was saying.

At the beginning of 1993 my husband was taken ill, and I had to return home to Zimbabwe. I stayed with my husband until he died. I returned to England to complete my studies with the intention of going back to Zimbabwe to be with my children, but the Lord had other plans. He told me to remain in England, to get a job and to get the children to come and join me.

Call to the down and out

Prayer continued to be my way of life, both with my friend and privately. But I felt increasingly that something was missing and I couldn't see quite what it was until I saw homeless people at the Bullring at Waterloo, London. I discovered that I had a burden for these people; so we started an outreach to the homeless. We visited them on Wednesdays with soup and sandwiches, and sometimes with hot meals prepared by the folk in our church. On Sundays we would collect some of them and bring them to the morning service. We would have a meal afterwards before taking them back to the city.

At this time I was going through a very difficult period in my personal life. It was proving to be problematic raising four children on a single nurse's salary and I was sinking into debt with every passing month. I was continually calling out to God for deliverance until one day the Lord said to me 'You have me to share your burden with. Look down your street and see how many single parents there are. They have nowhere to unburden their load and some of them are on the verge of suicide, drug addiction or of even abusing their children. Why don't you introduce them to me?'

That is how I started a ministry to single parents. Once a month we invited women and their children for a day out with the help of the youth team. We had a programme of sports, games, quizzes and some Bible stories, and we had discussion times on issues facing single parents – time and money management for example. We had times for testimonies, and at the end of the day every family would be prayed for. Mothers were able to pick up clothes and toys for their families which people from the church had donated as a result of this ministry. Many women made a commitment to the Lord.

Call to pray for Peckham

On one occasion while out shopping, I heard the words 'This is a desolate place, but if you believe and pray, I am going to change it into the garden of the Lord.' 'If it is you Lord' I said, 'confirm it with your word.' Then I heard the words from Isaiah 32:15. When I got home I checked it and this is what it says: 'Until the Spirit be poured upon us from on high, and the wilderness be a fruitful field, and the fruitful field be counted for a forest.'[1]

From that day I began to pray for Peckham. The Lord linked me together with ladies from the organization 'Women's Aglow' which also had a vision to evangelize the area. We met every week to pray for Peckham. During these times the Holy Spirit showed us that Peckham would be taken the way Jericho had been taken. We marked out some maps of the area and for six days we fasted and prayed over these maps. On the seventh day at midnight we literally walked and prayed around the whole area, shouting as we went. We then had victory celebrations into the early hours of the morning after returning to 'camp'.

At the end of that same year Peckham was allocated £64 million from the London Regeneration Programme for redevelopment. We witnessed the fall and destruction of derelict and depressing housing estates and the construction of beautiful new town houses. A new leisure centre has also been constructed and a space-age library is about to be completed. The word of God came to pass and the place has been transformed; it has become like the Garden of Eden. Every time we walk around Peckham we have been encouraged by the knowledge that we have a God who both hears and answers prayer.

Praying for the United Kingdom

'It is time to bring the church into the community, therefore go into the darkest part of the city and ignite my fire.' With these words the Lord challenged us to meet and pray in an ordinary community building and not in a church building or Christian home. So we hired a community hall with four other intercessors and met daily for 40 days for prayer and intercession with fasting, this time our focus being on the United Kingdom. We realized that there was an urgent need for an awakening of intercessors throughout the nation in order to pray for revival. The key scripture we took was Zechariah 3:3–10:

> Now Joshua was clothed with filthy garments, and stood before the angel.
> And he answered, and spake unto those that stood before him, saying, Take away the filthy garments from him. And unto him he said, Behold, I have caused thine iniquity to pass from thee, and I will clothe thee with change of raiment. And I said, Let them set a fair mitre upon his head. So they set a fair mitre upon his head, and clothed him with garments. And the angel of the LORD stood by. And the angel of the LORD protested unto Joshua, saying, Thus saith the LORD of hosts; If thou wilt walk in my ways, and if thou wilt keep my charge, then thou shalt also judge my house, and shalt also keep my courts, and I will give thee places to walk among these that stand by. Hear now, O Joshua the high priest, thou, and thy fellows that sit before thee: for they *are* men wondered at: for, behold, I will bring forth my servant the BRANCH. For behold the stone that I have laid before Joshua; upon one stone *shall be* seven eyes: behold, I will engrave the graving thereof, saith the LORD of hosts, and I will remove the iniquity of that land in one day. In that day, saith the LORD of hosts, shall ye call every man his neighbour under the vine and under the fig tree.

We felt that as a nation the United Kingdom needed to shed the filth of its iniquity from the highest levels of government, through all the ranks, to the ordinary people. We therefore repented for the sin of the nation, and prayed that the Lord would clothe the nation with righteousness and the fear of the Lord. There were four more days before the end of this period of prayer and it was during this time that I had what can be described as an encounter with the Lord.

Mission to Zimbabwe

Early on 4 January 1998 I was praying in my living room when the Lord appeared and stood opposite me. He looked glorious and his eyes were full of love. At first I was troubled, but soon all I felt was peace. He looked across into my eyes and said, 'What would you like me to do for you?' From deep within me I heard myself say 'Lord, that you would heal my country Zimbabwe', even though at that very moment in time I had been praying for the UK. 'I will send you for the healing of that nation' he replied, 'Me, Lord!' I answered, 'what can I do? All I know is how to pray.' He went on, 'I would like you to write a letter to President Mugabe to let him know that the situation in Zimbabwe is going to get worse. More people will die and the economy will continue to go down. This is because as a people you have sinned against God.'

He continued to show me the sin of Zimbabwe. The people have rejected God, pursued idolatry, the foreign gods of communism and Marxism. They had given glory to freedom fighters rather than God for the way they had won their independence as a nation. This had been reflected in the change of the national anthem.

He reminded me of the words from 2 Chronicles 7:14: 'If my people, which are called by my name, shall humble themselves, and pray, and seek my face, and turn from their wicked ways; then will I hear from heaven, and will forgive their sin, and will heal their land.' 'I would like you to call a national day of repentance. Tell your prayer partners to prepare to go to Zimbabwe in June.'

I was in shock for the whole of that day, and I was feeling very frightened. I shared what I had received with a workmate and she said to me, 'Elizabeth, if the Lord is challenging you to do this, he will do it for you, so trust him to do his word.' I remember that evening I was afraid to go into my prayer closet to pray. When I eventually did go in, the Holy Spirit continued to speak to me as if I had never left the room. He asked me to read the book of Nehemiah; I did this and when I got to the end of the second chapter, he said, 'Stop right there! And let's write that letter to the President.' So he dictated a letter to me, then I said, 'Lord, I have a letter but I do not have an address.' 'Phone the embassy and get the address.'

The following morning I phoned the embassy, and to my total surprise they gave me the president's address without asking any questions. I posted two identical letters, one by ordinary mail and the second by recorded mail. Twelve weeks later I received a reply from the president's office informing me that the president was also troubled by the plight of the nation. He hoped someone would rise up to do something about the matter (especially the plague of AIDS and HIV that was currently wreaking havoc on the land). On the strength of the president's response, the next challenge was how I could raise the money to travel there. It turned out that as I was in the process of changing jobs, my workmates at the time decided to give me some money to go and visit my parents in Zimbabwe. I was able to purchase the ticket to go home.

Once in Zimbabwe I went from one church leader to another trying to get support to mobilize the nation for a National Day of Prayer, but I was not getting any response. Nobody wanted to listen to me until, three days before I was due to leave for London, I met a gentleman who worked as a chaplain at a Christian college. During my discussion with him, he began to open to me what the Lord had been saying to me before I had told him anything. He later continued to encourage me by the words, 'You are hearing from God, and there are some intercessors who are also seeking to mobilize the Christians for a national day of repentance.' I was strengthened and keen to meet the people that he spoke of, so after getting their office address I went to visit them.

It turned out that the plans organized for the National Day of

Prayer and Repentance were identical to the plans that God had given me in Britain. According to the pattern in the book of Nehemiah, the people were to stand in their communities and repent for the sins of their home, village, city and nation. I was very encouraged knowing that I had heard from the Lord after all, and that the plan was in motion. The 25th of May 1998 was the date that had been set for this National Day of Repentance.

After I got back to England, however, I was restless and upset with God – why had he asked me to arrange a National Day of Prayer when he had already appointed someone in the nation to do it? God spoke to me with the words, 'I asked you to prepare the mission to Zimbabwe for June, so continue to seek my face.' So I continued to seek the face of the Lord. He led me to invite all the church leaders and departmental leaders in the church to a one-day conference at the Harare International Conference Centre, Zimbabwe. This was like asking me to invite church leaders in the UK for a conference at the Ritz! Where was I to get the money from to embark on such a venture? I decided to trust and follow the leading of the Holy Spirit.

The chaplain whom I had met earlier helped us with the database from the Christian college, through which we were able to send invitations to church leaders from the different cities in the country. In faith, we also booked the conference centre at the Harare Sheraton. Candidates were coming from far-off places, and we felt that the Lord wanted us to supply them with lunch. So the challenges continued to mount up. We continued to prepare for this conference not really knowing what it was to be all about. I remember saying to the Lord one day, 'What is to be the name of the mission?' He responded by asking me, 'What is the name of the car that I gave you, which you have been driving around?' I responded with sudden realization, 'TRIUMPH!' 'That is what the mission shall be called. It *has* been a command for your life, it *is* a command to Zimbabwe, to Africa and to the nations.' So I studied all the scriptures that mentioned 'Triumph'.

- *Triumph* over sin represented by Egypt:
  Exodus 15:1b–2: 'I will sing unto the LORD, for he hath

triumphed gloriously: the horse and his rider hath he thrown into the sea. The LORD is my strength and song, and he is become my salvation: he is my God, and I will prepare him an habitation; my father's God, and I will exalt him.'
- *Triumph* over my enemies throughout my salvation journey represented by Moab and Edom. Psalm 60:8a: 'Moab *is* my washpot; over Edom will I cast out my shoe . . . triumph thou.' Moab and Edom were a challenge to Israel during her journey to the Promised Land.
- *Triumph* over the giants in my heritage represented by Philistine. Psalm 60:8b: 'Over Philistia, triumph thou (Israel) because of me.' Philistines were a challenge to Israel in the land of promise.

As I studied I began to understand the meaning of 2 Corinthians 2:14: 'Now thanks be unto God, which always causeth us to triumph in Christ, and maketh manifest the savour of his knowledge by us in every place.' With only four days left before making the trip to Harare, the Lord gave me a word for the nation from Isaiah 40:1–5:

> Comfort ye, comfort ye my people, saith your God. Speak ye comfortably to Jerusalem, and cry unto her, that her warfare is accomplished, that her iniquity is pardoned: for she hath received of the LORD's hand double for all her sins. The voice of him that crieth in the wilderness, Prepare ye the way of the LORD, make straight in the desert a highway for our God. Every valley shall be exalted, and every mountain and hill shall be made low: and the crooked shall be made straight, and the rough places plain: And the glory of the LORD shall be revealed, and all flesh shall see *it* together: for the mouth of the LORD hath spoken it.

It seemed that the Lord was responding to the many prayers of repentance made on 25 May. Just as he had appointed someone to gather the people for repentance, he was also recruiting someone who would deliver his response. He was saying to Zimbabwe, 'Be comforted because your sin has been forgiven.'

Though we had sinned terribly and suffered as a result of it, the Lord had forgiven us as a nation. Our struggle was to come to an end. Even though our economy is in shambles, AIDS is on the increase and corruption is rampant, yet the Lord was sending a voice to cry out in that wilderness to prepare the way of the Lord. He was going to pour out his Spirit upon his people, and they would begin to prophesy to every situation that was confronting the whole nation. The solutions to our problems would not come from the government and from foreign aid; neither would they come from human wisdom. Instead they would come through the word and Spirit of the Lord working among his people.

The Church was being challenged to spend more time waiting on the Lord so that he could counsel and empower us for the task that lay ahead. Five hundred Christian leaders arrived for that conference. It was a unique day in our history, first because it was a woman who was bringing the prophetic word to the nation, and second because the people wept as they realized that the plans that God had for us were to bring us to a perfect end (see Jeremiah 29:11), and not destruction as currently painted.

For five days following the conference, we carried this prophetic word to all of the provinces in the nation. By the grace of God we were able to meet with mayors and provincial governors who in turn called departmental leaders to hear the word of the Lord for the nation and to receive prayer for themselves, their people and their community.

A voice crying in the wilderness

When I got back to England I went back to work as a midwife and continued to enjoy my fellowship with the Holy Spirit and my prayer times with my colleagues. After six weeks the Lord visited me again, this time in Surrey where I happened to be working, and asked me the question, 'Could you do something for me?' 'What would you like me to do?' I responded with a hint of suspicion. 'Could you be my voice crying out in the wilderness?' he answered. In retrospect, the first mission was very successful, but every move was by faith, and we were tested on every side. All that was accomplished had nothing to do with any of those who participated. We were just vessels available for the Master's use. We had no money in our pockets. None of us had previous missionary experience to draw upon. Now in view of this I knew what it meant to be in a wilderness, and I was not at all keen to yield to this particular call. So I said, 'Lord if you want me to do this, you have to make my heart willing to do it.'

Within about two weeks my attitude was totally different. I was now very eager to go to Zimbabwe and to do the will of God. Again his instructions seemed very clear. 'I would like you to go and preach in every city in that nation the word that I am going to put in your mouth. You will be away for six weeks.' Now at this time I was still working and I knew that it would not be possible to take time off for a holiday. I was also concerned about how my children would survive if I gave up my job, not to mention how bills would be paid. I had many questions. The Lord reminded me, 'The children belong to me, remember you entrusted them to me in 1994.' So in spite of all these constraints and concerns I knew that I was going to obey the call.

I gave up my job; I left the children with my sister and travelled to Zimbabwe with virtually no money in my pocket. While there, I travelled to twenty cities, preaching from Isaiah 60. I was even able to fly to Victoria Falls (for ministry): that is how lavishly the Lord supplied my needs during that mission. The Lord wanted me to inform the nation of the glory that was going to be revealed, that Zimbabwe had a significant role to play in God's great plan for the whole continent of Africa and other nations. Also, that he had a plan for the restoration of all the people, from those in government to the ordinary people on the street. This restoration would affect us spiritually, emotionally, physically and economically.

He also asked me to challenge the church leaders to rise up and to mobilize their churches to look after the widows and orphans in their regions. God was reminding us that he had given gifts to individuals and not just to congregations (Ephesians 4:8). The Lord was saying that the pastors had been raised up to care for their communities and not just for their congregations. Every wise pastor should know the state of their flock (Proverbs 27:23); therefore the Lord will require an accounting of the communities in which he has placed pastors.

The strategy that I was given for the Church with regard to looking after widows and orphans was based on two scriptures. The first is from Genesis 41:34–35. It is part of the story of Joseph just before he was governor of the land, and just after he had interpreted Pharaoh's dreams.

> Let Pharaoh do this, and let him appoint officers over the land, and take up the fifth part of the land of Egypt in the seven plenteous years. And let them gather all the food of those good years that come, and lay up corn under the hand of Pharaoh, and let them keep food in the cities.

The second is from Acts 6:1–7:

> And in those days, when the number of the disciples was multiplied, there arose a murmuring of the Grecians against the Hebrews, because their widows were neglected in the daily ministration. Then the twelve called the multitude of the disciples unto them, and said, It is not reason that we should leave the word of God, and serve tables. Wherefore, brethren, look ye out among you seven men of honest report, full of the Holy Ghost and wisdom, whom we may appoint over this business. But we will give ourselves continually to prayer, and to the ministry of the word. And the saying pleased the whole multitude: and they chose Stephen, a man full of faith and of the Holy Ghost, and Philip, and Prochorus, and Nicanor, and Timon, and Parmenas, and Nicolas a proselyte of Antioch: Whom they set before the apostles: and when they had prayed, they laid their hands on them. And the word of God increased; and the number of the disciples multiplied in Jerusalem greatly; and a great company of the priests were obedient to the faith.

Through these passages it became clear that God was calling the Church:

1. to be involved in the life of its community;
2. to appoint spirit-filled men and women of integrity to look into the affairs and needs of the community;
3. to build storehouses in the church, where members could contribute food and clothing items from their personal shopping or whatever harvest is reaped, to be distributed to these needy families;
4. to allocate foster parents over the orphans to look into their spiritual, emotional and physical development under the supervision of the church, so that each child was able to relate to somebody within the church;
5. 'Children and Youth Development and Training' days in the church were to be organized on regular occasions.

I know now that intercession is not just prayer and spending time groaning, but it involves receiving wisdom from God and moving forward in the light of that instruction. Intercession is going to God on behalf of the people, bringing their needs before God and receiving from him, and when you have received you bring to the people. Joel puts it like this:

> Let the priests, the ministers of the LORD, weep between the porch and the altar, and let them say, Spare thy people, O LORD, and give not thine heritage to reproach, that the heathen should rule over them: wherefore should they say among the people, Where is their God? Then will the LORD be jealous for his land, and pity his people. Yea, the LORD will answer and say unto his people, Behold, I will send you corn, and wine, and oil, and ye shall be satisfied therewith: and I will no more make you a reproach among the heathen: But I will remove far off from you the northern army, and will drive him into a land barren and desolate, with his face toward the east sea, and his hinder part toward the utmost sea, and his stink shall come up, and his ill savour shall come up, because he hath done great things. Fear not, O land; be glad and rejoice: for the LORD will do great things. (Joel 2:17–21)

An effective prayer life comes from a relationship with God. We need to realize that he is with us continually; we have an ongoing relationship with him. Also that he takes us from strength to strength, from glory to glory and as a Father he leads us step by step: from praying for your church, to praying for your street: from praying for your community, to your borough, then to your city; to your nation and then praying for the nations of the earth.

Since my first mission to Zimbabwe two years ago I have made six mission trips, and planted prayer cells in 21 cities which are multiplying each month. TRIUMPH is actively involved in the storehouse programmes in the Zambezi valley, Masvingo and in Harare. A programme is in operation to mobilize the Church in the challenge of looking after widows and orphans through training pastors and teaching believers to give. I am now involved in planning a 'TRIUMPH AFRICA' conference in London where we are inviting Christians of African origin from Britain and Europe to hear the hope for Africa and give them strategies for the deliverance of their nations.

Notes

1 All Bible quotations are taken from the King James Version unless otherwise stated.

PRAYER AND DECISION-MAKING

Cebert Richards

> Bishop Cebert Thomas Richards is the National Overseer of the Church of Jesus Christ Apostolic, England. He is also the pastor of the local church in Sheffield where he currently resides. He has received a Bachelor's degree in Theology and is also a Doctor in Divinity. He is a counsellor and works closely with the education and social services departments in Sheffield. He is now a retired Education Welfare Officer whose remit was to work as a counsellor and offer support to disruptive pupils. Recently he has become a member of the Churches Regional Commission for Yorkshire and Humberside and also the Regional Chamber for Yorkshire and Humberside.

God in his infinite grace and mercy from the beginning of time has made a way whereby he can communicate with humanity and therefore have a relationship through prayer. So the foundation of prayer is in the nature of God; he is love. 'And we have known and believed the love that God hath to us. God is love; and he that dwelleth in love dwelleth in God, and God in him' (1 John 4:16).[1] God has created for himself creatures that will communicate with him. Prayer is universal, for it was God's intention that all people should come to him.

> Also the sons of the stranger, that join themselves to the LORD, to serve him, and to love the name of the LORD, to be his servants, every one that keepeth the Sabbath from polluting it, and taketh hold of my covenant. Even them will I bring to my holy mountain, and make them joyful in my house of prayer: their burnt offerings and their sacrifices shall be accepted upon mine altar; for mine house shall be called an house of prayer for all people. (Isaiah 56:6–7)

God created humans as temporal and weak, needing him: 'And to Seth, to him also there was born a son; and he called his name Enos: then began men to call upon the name of the LORD' (Genesis 4:26). Also see Psalm 90:1–12.

So as believers in Christ Jesus, for us to make decisions which affect not only our own lives but also others, we must seek to know what the will of God is in general, and God's will for us as individuals. When the disciples of Jesus came to him and enquired about the way to pray, Jesus told them:

> Our Father which art in heaven, Hallowed be thy name. Thy kingdom come. Thy will be done in earth, as it is in heaven. Give us this day our daily bread. And forgive us our debts, as we forgive our debtors. And lead us not into temptation, but deliver us from evil: For thine is the kingdom, and the power, and the glory, for ever. Amen. (Matthew 6:9–13)

Special notice should be taken of verse 10 which states, 'Thy kingdom come, thy will be done on earth as it is in heaven.'

In Luke 11:1 Jesus said to his disciples, 'After this manner therefore pray ye.' Jesus gave this as a model prayer after one of his disciples said to him, 'Lord, teach us to pray, as John also taught his disciples.' We are to pray to our Father who is in heaven, because he is all-wise, all-loving and all-powerful. We are also instructed to pray in the name of Jesus. 'And whatsoever ye shall ask in my name, that will I do, that the Father may be glorified in the Son. If ye shall ask any thing in my name, I will do it' (John 14:13–14).

Prayer depends upon the mediative influence of the Holy Spirit:

> Likewise the Spirit also helpeth our infirmities: for we know not what we should pray for as we ought: but the Spirit itself maketh intercession for us with groanings which cannot be uttered. And he that searcheth the hearts knoweth what is the mind of the Spirit, because he maketh intercession for the saints according to the will of God. (Romans 8:26–27)

The model prayer is brief, to the point and not repetitive: it is the perfect prayer. If we observe what prayer is, we will understand that it is talking to God, it is asking and receiving. It is making your request known to him in faith. Because the scripture presents prayer so simply, we are in danger of failing to recognize its immensity. Our Lord instructed the believers to ask, seek and knock, because these words cover the whole spectrum of prayer.

Prayer is asking and receiving. When you know the will of God regarding a need, whether it is natural or spiritual, you can ask and receive. This prayer is according to the will of God. 'And this is the confidence that we have in him, that, if we ask any thing according to his will, he heareth us: And if we know that he hear us, whatsoever we ask, we know that we have the petitions that we desired of him' (1 John 5:14–15).

Prayer is seeking and finding. When you know the will of God regarding a need, whether it be material or spiritual, then you are to seek this need until you find it. This is prayer for a knowledge of the unrevealed will of God in a specific need. 'If ye then be risen with Christ, seek those things which are above, where Christ sitteth on the right hand of God' (Colossians 3:1). 'Then shall ye call upon me, and ye shall go and pray unto me, and I will hearken unto you. And ye shall seek me, and find me, when ye shall search for me with all your heart' (Jeremiah 29:12–13).

Prayer is knocking and opening. When you know the will of God, and yet you find a closed door, you are to knock and keep on knocking until God opens the door. This is a tenacious prayer for mountain-moving faith.

> And Jesus said unto them, Because of your unbelief: for verily I say unto you, If ye have faith as a grain of mustard seed, ye shall say unto this mountain, Remove hence to yonder place; and it shall remove; and nothing shall be impossible unto you. Howbeit this kind goeth not out but by prayer and fasting. (Matthew 17:14–21)

All things are possible when you ask, seek and knock within the will of God. If we look closely into the will of God, we will discover that God has a sovereign will, a moral will and an individual will.

Sovereign will of God

The sovereign will of God can be defined as God's predetermined plan for everything that happens in the universe. When we say that God is sovereign, we are saying that he is the almighty ruler of the universe, that in eternity God formulates a perfect plan for all history. He determines how nations will act and how kings, rulers and governments will rule. The world was created by his will: he spoke and it was done and our salvation through Jesus Christ is the result of God working all things after the counsel of his sovereign will.

The moral will of God

The moral will is defined as God's moral commands that are revealed in the Bible through the written word teaching humanity how they ought to believe, live and make decisions. Jesus said 'And all things, whatsoever ye shall ask in prayer, believing, ye shall receive' (Matthew 21:22). So as we examine the scriptures and study them we can clearly see that the Bible reveals a hundred per cent of God's moral will. For this reason the apostle Paul stated in Romans 2 that the unbelieving Jews knew God's will because they had the scriptures, or the written word of God. They knew right from wrong because they knew the moral will of God. In some instances a specific command is said to be God's moral will, for example the word of God confirms in 1 Thessalonians 5:18 'In every thing give thanks: for this is the will of God in Christ Jesus concerning you.' So the Bible contains general instructions which affect all our lives, but do not determine each decision we make. Instructions can be found in the word of God as it was given to the children of Israel on tablets of stone. So, as we read the Bible the moral will of God will be revealed to us through his word.

The individual will of God

Let us try to define God's individual will. I believe it is that ideal, detailed life-plan which God has uniquely designed for each believer. This life-plan encompasses every decision we make and is the basis of God's daily guidance in our decision-making. This guidance is given through the indwelling of the Holy Spirit who progressively reveals God's life-plan to the heart of the individual believer.

The Spirit of God uses many means to reveal this life-plan, as we shall see. He always gives confirmation at the point of each decision-making. It is important to live as a dedicated believer and make one's decision within the larger circle of God's moral will, but finding that which God requires of us as individuals is essential in making correct decisions in our daily lives.

In seeking to fulfil our goals in decision-making we cannot forget the word of our Lord and Saviour Jesus Christ in his teachings, 'Ask, and it shall be given you; seek, and ye shall find; knock, and it shall be opened unto you: For every one that asketh receiveth; and he that seeketh findeth; and to him that knocketh it shall be opened' (Matthew 7:7–8).

This process can only be achieved through prayer. So the way to be certain to find God's individual will for each believer is through prayer. Some believers constantly say that they cannot find or know the will of God, forgetting the words of God in Acts 1:8, 'But ye shall receive power, after that the Holy Ghost is come upon you: and ye shall be witnesses unto me both in Jerusalem, and in all Judea, and in Samaria, and unto the uttermost part of the earth', and forgetting that we can do all things through 'Christ who strengthens us'.

God's individual will is known through personal communication with God. It is frustrating to attempt to read a sign that is just a bit too far away, or to try to understand the words of someone who is slightly out of hearing range. In personal relationships distance also affects communication; when we say that a husband and wife are distant from each other, we mean they are not enjoying marriage communion with each other. If this is the case, then the lack of marriage communion will inevitably lead to a lack of marriage communication. On the other hand, it is a delight to watch a husband and wife who have grown in their love and communion through the years. They communicate on a level that would be unknown by other couples who merely lived at the same address. Often one spouse can sense how his or her partner feels about a matter without even having to ask. Such people are able to communicate with each other with the slightest squeeze of the hand, the smallest facial expression, or even a certain glance of the eye. Such is the level of communication that is desired by the Lord, who is our personal guide. God desires that our communion with him be so close that even the slightest glance of his eye will communicate his will to us.

In Psalm 32:8, God says 'I will instruct thee and teach thee in the way which thou shalt go: I will guide thee with mine eye.' This type of guidance requires close communion that has no need of the bit and bridle required by animals such as horses and mules. 'Be ye not as the horse, or as the mule, which have no understanding: whose mouth must be held in with bit and bridle, lest they come near unto thee' (Psalm 32:9). Such guidance as this is possible only when we are close to the Lord. When our fellowship is so intimate that we are walking by his side, then we will be aware of the slightest communication from the Holy Spirit.

Regardless of that which we can have, or that which we are able to achieve, nothing replaces closeness to the Lord – not formulae, not books on God's will, not going to seminars to be lectured or taught about God's will, not college or Bible school degrees, not even perfect church attendance. The closer you are to God, the closer you will be to finding certainty in the knowledge of his will. Sometimes, because of our busy schedules, we cannot quite hear or see God's leading. Draw closer to him and be assured that as you make the move, he will draw closer to you as well. 'Draw nigh to God, and he will draw nigh to you. Cleanse your hands, ye sinners; and purify your hearts, ye double minded. Be afflicted, and mourn, and weep: let your laughter be turned to mourning, and your joy to heaviness. Humble yourselves in the sight of the Lord, and he shall lift you up' (James 4:8–10).

I am convinced that 99 per cent of those who cannot find God's will are not spending enough time in prayer. If we do not ask God, we will not receive: 'Ye lust, and have not: ye kill, and desire to have, and cannot obtain: ye fight and war, yet ye have not, because ye ask not' (James 4:2), and so it will be very difficult to make the right decisions.

How many hours did you pray this week? If believers spent as much time praying for God's will as they do frantically looking for it, most of our problems would be eliminated.

The next time you are tempted to take an hour to go and purchase a book on God's will, stay at home and spend the time on your knees. Prayer is like a clean windshield when you are seeking God's will: it allows you to see the road and the signs clearly without distortion or distraction. Prayer is like a rush of cool air from a rolled-down window. It brings the drowsy driver back to full alertness. Therefore, he can make the decisions which are necessary for that time, place, situation and circumstance.

Godly saints will always tell you that the inward witness of the Holy Spirit is most clearly heard when they are quiet before God in prayer. It is then that his still, small voice can be clearly heard. It is not drowned out with the noisiness and busy-ness of our lives. If we look deeply into prayer and decision-making we will find that many believers, if they are honest, admit that it is hard for them to get started in prayer; and even once they have begun, the slightest distraction seems to cut it short. It may be hard to continue and wait in prayer, but it is even harder to live a life after missing God's individual will from lack of prayer. If you pray and the answer does not come immediately, wait before God until it does. It may be that he is using this decision to get your undivided attention; if you will wait before him in prayer, the answer will come and it will not be too late. So let prayer stimulate your alertness to the signs, cultivate your ability to hear the still, small voice, and develop your attentiveness to God. By doing so you will be confident in decision-making.

After looking through the various ways of the will of God and how that relates to our decision-making, it now remains for us to see how these observations relate to the process of decision-making in particular. How is God involved in this important aspect of our lives? And how do we, as the children of God, respond to him as we apply the principles of his moral will and wisdom to our decisions?

According to the Bible, God is involved in our decision-making at several levels.

1. He has provided the resources for making decisions that are acceptable to him. He has instructed us in his word to seek wisdom for making decisions, and has informed us how to do it. Further, he has given us a new nature, which makes obedience of his moral will possible. As a loving father he has equipped us with everything we need to make decisions that are pleasing to him. As we work through the process of arriving at a decision, God is continually present and working within us by his Spirit. The words of the apostle Paul remind us 'For it is God which worketh in you, both to will and to do of his good pleasure' (Philippians 2:13).

    Specifically, his grace enables us to trust him. 'And when he was disposed to pass into Achaia, the brethren wrote exhorting the disciples to receive him: who, when he was come, helped them much which had believed through grace' (Acts 18:27).

    He helps the believer to obey his will and by his Spirit he provides the opportunity to keep his commandments, so every single act of obedience is proof of God's involvement in our lives. 'For they that are after the flesh do mind the things of the flesh; but they that are after the Spirit the things of the Spirit. For to be carnally minded is death; but to be spiritually minded is life and peace. Because the carnal mind is enmity against God: for it is not subject to the law of God, neither indeed can be. So then they that are in the flesh cannot please God' (Romans 8:5–8).
2. Furthermore, it is God whose sovereignty opens doors of opportunity for us. When we ask for wisdom, he gives it through the channels he has established for our benefit. He also answers the related prayers we offer concerning our decisions, and he brings to successful completion those of

our plans that are within his sovereign will. In all this, God utilizes the circumstances and the very process of decision-making to change our character and bring us to maturity as we depend on him and he blesses our obedience to his moral will and produces his spiritual fruit in our lives.

3. He works through our decisions to accomplish his purpose not only *in* us but also *through* us, so that others can also be recipients of those decisions that we make. My primary response to these objectively revealed truths is to be one of trust in God. Trust is actualized by thinking, feeling and acting as though everything God says about himself is true. Such trust is expressed in a variety of ways. It is expressed in my confidence that God exercises control over all things, and without him I can do nothing. It is manifested in my prayer for open doors, and in my expectation that he is working all things together for good, 'And we know that all things work together for good to them that love God, to them who are the called according to his purpose' (Romans 8:28). This is my response to his sovereign guidance and assurance that all things are in him and for him.

I demonstrate faith when I conscientiously obey what I understand of God's moral will, and seek to apply the principles of God's word to my decision. I express trust when I take seriously God's intention that decisions within the area of my freedom are to be made by me. This is my response to his moral guidance that I can achieve that which I need within the written word of God as stated in the Bible.

Trust is expressed in my prayers for wisdom as I approach the decision at hand, and my careful pursuit and evaluation of the wisdom sources he has provided reflect my confidence in the reliability of the pattern he has prescribed. This is my response to his wisdom guidance: 'If any of you lack wisdom, let him ask of God, that giveth to all men liberally, and upbraideth not; and it shall be given him. But let him ask in faith, nothing wavering' (James 1:5-6a). Finally, I express trust when I thank him in advance for what he is going to accomplish through the decision-making process as well as the outcome of the decision itself.

This is my response to the reality of his presence and involvement in my life. We have seen that God is thoroughly involved at every level of the process of decision-making and how he manifests himself and his will to the believer to the extent and nature of his participation in believers' lives. So the resolution lies in recognizing that 'we walk by faith and not by sight' (2 Corinthians 5:7).

So in making decisions in our Christian lives, in many areas we affect others, as well as ourselves. We must seek God and his acknowledgement because it is through his will that we are able to make these decisions, as he taught his disciples to pray, 'Thy will be done in earth as it is in heaven.'

Be enveloped by his divine will through prayer and decision-making, and his richest blessings enfold you all.

Note

1 All scripture references are taken from King James Version.

PRAYING IN THE SPIRIT

Philip Mohabir

Philip Mohabir was born in Guyana and at the age of fifteen became the only Christian in his Hindu village. After eight years in England as a missionary in the 1950s and 1960s, he returned to his homeland with his wife Muriel whom he met in England, and for nineteen years pioneered in evangelism and church planting throughout Guyana and the Caribbean, establishing over 100 churches. Since moving to the UK in 1983 he has been committed to building bridges between black and white Christians, and is the founder and first President of the African and Caribbean Evangelical Alliance (ACEA). He oversees the International Christian Leadership Connections (ICLC) Network and leads the UK-based Connections ministry. His book *Building Bridges* and the video *Philip Mohabir – Fisher of Men* tells his story. His mandate: 'Take the gospel of Christ to the different people.'

Rediscovering the prayer dynamic

Prayer is a lost art that is waiting to be rediscovered by the Church. The secret of the early Church's success was the quality of its prayer life. When the people prayed, great things happened. Fire fell down from heaven, thousands were converted, buildings shook, miracles, signs, wonders were very much in evidence. Prison doors swung wide open, demons fled, towns and villages were turned upside down. Whole cities and continents were powerfully impacted.

In the first century the early Church crashed into history and it shaped and changed the destiny of the whole known world. It has never been the same since. The manifest presence and power of the risen Christ was an ever-present reality. The demonstration of the supernatural was natural to them. The extraordinary and miraculous were normal to their everyday experience. There was a certain dynamic in their practice of prayer that is sadly missing in today's Church. Our mission now is no less demanding than theirs. Every believer and church needs to reassess the effectiveness of their own prayer lives. If, like them, we too are called to penetrate the heavens, touch the throne of grace and intercede to see the hand of God revealed in power, then we must learn how to pray in the Spirit like they did. We need to recapture the Holy Spirit dimension in prayer. If the Church is to fulfil its prophetic role in the twenty-first-century world, then *we* must experience afresh something more of the authority, life and power of the first-century Church.

Prayer and the paraclete

The prayer of the Christian believer is distinct and vastly different from others. The Holy Spirit, the third person of the godhead, is directly involved. He indwells the believer to make him or her alive to God. He initiates and sustains that contact with God. Effective prayer should be Spirit-led, directed and energized. Unlike other religions, Christian prayer is not cluttered by religious paraphernalia, endless rituals, complicated forms and sophistication. Prayer for the child of God is meant to be an honest heart-to-heart talk to his or her Father. It is giving yourself space and time to open up your heart to him; to share your deepest feeling, to reveal your innermost secrets and cherished thoughts without fear of embarrassment or betrayal, to communicate the kind of things you cannot confidentially share with anyone. It is like the hour that Adam had with God in the cool of the day in the garden before the fall. The Holy Spirit specializes in creating that hallowed environment right in the midst of all our pressurized situations and brings us to meet with God face to face. However, there is a condition. We must make time to draw near to seek him. There is a place of quiet rest near to the heart of God. *The Holy Spirit helps our weakness* (Romans 8:26).

I admit that we, mere fallen mortals, find it very difficult to switch off our overactive mind and to find regular time to retreat from our daily routine. We need supernatural help: the Spirit is that promised Helper. He will not take over our responsibility but will draw alongside us to give us a helping hand. He helps us carry the load whatever our weakness. Our weaknesses in prayer can range from any or all of the following:

- Lack of determination.
- Lack of strength, energy, apathy and inertia.
- Lack of confidence and a general feeling of failure.
- Sense of inadequacy and vulnerability.
- Feeling of hopelessness and helpless despair.
- Feeling of low self-esteem and unworthiness.
- Suffering from guilt complex and condemnation.
- Tendency to give in to doubts and depression.
- Inability to carry the load or bear the burden alone.

Tiredness and sickness can wear us down, but none of these things is beyond the ability of the Spirit to help us. He is more than able to deliver us and bring us into victory. However, it must be pointed out that the Spirit does not help us to harbour doubt, distrust or disobedience. These are sins which must be confessed in order to be forgiven and cleansed (Proverbs 28:13; 1 John 1:9). Praying in the Spirit is allowing God to work in us so that he can pray through us.

Keep it simple

Jesus taught his disciples that true prayers should be uncomplicated, rooted in reality and free from all embellishment (Matthew 6), with simplicity and spontaneity being major hallmarks. Our heavenly Father invites us to enter his throne-room: not because of our righteousness but solely on the merit of the shed blood of Jesus. He bids us come boldly, not in fear – as his children, not as slaves. We have received the Spirit of Son-ship. In John 1:12 we are told that as many as receive Jesus and believe on his name he gives them the authority and the right to be the children of God, 'The Spirit Himself bears witness with our spirit that we are the children of God' (Romans 8:14–16).

The nature of Christian prayer is indeed unique. In its object, purpose and scope it stands splendidly and incomparably alone. *Our* object is the mighty omnipotent God who is our loving heavenly Father. *Our* purpose is holy worship, redemptive welfare and victorious warfare. *Our* scope reaches into heavenly realms, impacts planet earth and affects the kingdom of darkness. The humble believer prays having this assurance that:

- he/she is accepted by his grace;
- the name of Jesus is his/her authority;
- the blood of Jesus is his/her guarantee;
- the Holy Spirit [Paraclete] is his/her helper;
- the word of God is his/her sure bedrock foundation that underpins his/her faith.

In contrast, although people of all religions engage in some form of prayer, they have no assurance that their prayers will be heard by the true and living God. Like the prophets of Baal they call in vain (1 Kings 18:20–26).

Holy Spirit power versus powers of darkness

There are external and internal enemies. The Church is pitched in battle against the gates of hell. Prince demons are in direct confrontation to the children of God: lambs sent to conquer wolves. The first disciples of Jesus realized that not all prayers are effective even if they are sincere. This is why they asked the Lord to teach them how to pray (Luke 11:1). Jesus said, 'When you pray do not pray as the hypocrites, do not pray as the Gentiles' (Matthew 6:5, 7). The apostle Paul knew that not every and any kind of prayer would prevail. Why? Because we wrestle not against flesh and blood but against rulers, powers and principalities, against the forces of darkness and against spiritual forces of wickedness in the heavenly places (Ephesians 6:12). The Church is called to warfare. The Church is called to war that necessitates the Holy Spirit engagement.

The Church is the sole appointed agency that is called to confront the powers of hell, pull down satanic strongholds and set captives held in bondage of sin and evil free. The Lord knew that as ordinary human beings we do not have what it takes to defeat Satan, therefore he has given us the Holy Spirit to 'help our weakness; for we do not know how to pray as we should, but the Spirit Himself intercedes for us with groaning too deep for words' (Romans 8:26). 'Groaning in the Spirit' is a description of a level of intensity in prayer far beyond any human capability – a supernatural exercise that can only be reproduced in us by the Spirit. It really does not matter how intelligent we are or how well formed our prayers are theologically. We may pray loudly or silently, we may read set prayers or we can be spontaneous. We can shout religious jargon as often and as loudly as we want, repeat them again and again. We can hype it up or go in the silent, quiet syndrome. The form and style are not what matters. Human intelligence and ingenuity do not shift evil spiritual forces. We need to discover how to plumb the depths in prayer in the power of the Holy Spirit.

The believers at Corinth had to struggle against demonic attacks, divisions, immorality, power struggles, theological differences and abuse of spiritual gifts. They were persecuted from within and without. It looked very confusing and chaotic. Against this background Paul exhorted them to look beyond the obvious and tackle the problems at the very heart. Behind most of our problems is a real devil at work. He said,

> Though we walk in the flesh, we do not war according to the flesh, for the weapons of our warfare are not of the flesh but mighty in God for the pulling [destruction] of strongholds, casting down arguments and every high thing that exalts itself against the knowledge of God, bringing every thought into captivity to the knowledge of Christ. (2 Corinthians 10:3–5)

The weapons of the Spirit are provided for us to do battle against evil spirits, contrived and controlled opposition. In an age when culture is rapidly changing, the Church must rise to a new place of apostolic authority in order to remain relevant in a highly apostate generation. Prayer cannot be regarded as a personal devotional exercise only, neither can it be relegated to the midweek duty of a dedicated handful, but it must become the work and ministry of the entire Church. Prayer as a casual, cosy pastime will not suffice. The challenges of our age require consistent and persistent corporate effort. Prayer that is charged with the dynamism of the Spirit must be the priority and passionate pursuit of every Christian.

Prayer points to ponder
- Prayer is as essential to the inner spiritual person as breathing is to the physical.
- Prayer is a privilege of grace, not a religious duty to gain points.
- A prayerful people is a powerful people, but a prayerless people is a powerless people.
- A travailing Church is a prevailing Church.
- Weeping may endure for a night, but joy comes in the morning.
- The falling tears of prayer now in time never fall forgotten, they are stored in eternity.
- The weakest believer engaged in prayer on his/her knees constitutes a threat to the devil.
- More things are wrought by prayer than this world dreams of.
- Prayer is essential to all Christian service.
- The kingdom of God on earth advances on knees bowed in prayer.

Praying in the Spirit is praying in harmony with the will of God

We cannot make God do what he has decided not to do, but we can command him to do what he has already decided to do. Praying in the Spirit is discerning what God already wants to do and then praying accordingly. If our hearts are set on the kingdom of God and if we hunger after righteousness, the Holy Spirit will reveal God's heart and will to us (Matthew 6:33). As Jesus prayed in the Garden of Gethsemane, in great agony he enquired, 'Father if it is possible, let this cup pass from me.' After many agonizing, soul-searching moments eventually he surrendered his own will and submitted himself to the will of his

Father. 'Not as I will but as you will.' Again after the third time he said, 'Your will be done' (Matthew 26:36–42). The great apostle Peter had a great inner soul conflict when he was praying in Joppa. God was asking him to do something that was diametrically opposed to his upbringing, his understanding of scripture and his culture. In desperation he cried out, 'Not so, Lord!' (Acts 10:9–48). We know the rest of the story: a revival broke out among the Gentiles as a result of his giving up on his own preconceptions and bowing to the will of God.

Contemporary society conditions us to be fiercely independent and self-centred. The desires of our heart pull us away from God's plans. We become so obsessed with our own needs, desires and ambitions that we do not leave room or place for what God wants with our lives. We want God to give us what we want, what we think is best for us. When we earnestly seek the Lord in prayer, the Holy Spirit will bring to the surface all the hidden things that conflict with the will of God. He will further challenge and convict us to surrender them and submit ourselves to the rule of Christ until we cry, 'Your will be done.' Jesus knows how difficult it is for us to rightly discern the mind and will of God. He also knows that even when we understand what pleases him, we find it difficult to fully accept it and totally submit to it. In our own strength it is impossible, but the Spirit is given to us for our benefit. He is sent to enlighten and empower us to do all that he desires. Jesus said, 'When He the Spirit of truth has come He will guide you into all truth; for He will not speak of His own authority, but whatever He hears He will speak. He will glorify Me, He will take of what is mine and declare it to you' (John 16:12–15).

As we wait on God in prayer, we give the Spirit opportunity to work in our hearts in order to clear away all resistance or ignorance concerning his will.

> For the Spirit searches all things, yes, the deep things of God. For what man knows the spirit of a man except the spirit of the man which is in him? Even so no one knows the things of God except the Spirit of God. Now we have received not the spirit of the world, but the Spirit who is

from God, that we might know the things that have been freely given us from God. (1 Corinthians 2:10–12)

When our hearts are in harmony with God's heart, the way is opened for the Lord to answer our prayers and fight our battles. If we allow him, then there is absolutely nothing too hard for God.

Praying in the Spirit is to operate under the inspiration of the Spirit

Praying is not just speaking but is also listening: it is a two-way thing. We all tend to make a common mistake – we seem to be in too much of a hurry to tell God everything we can, to give him a list of requests. We leave very little time for meditation and contemplation. Listening and reflecting on what the Spirit says is as essential as our words. It is important to come expecting the Spirit to speak, fill us with his presence and transport us away from the ordinary, everyday things: the noise, hatred, confusion and a million voices all clamouring for our attention. Create time to be alone with God. Let us come apart and invite the Spirit to imbue us with his peace, love and joy. Prayer can be a dull, regimental discipline instead of a voluntary joyous exhilarating time. It need not be such a burden and drudgery to pray. We do not have to be cold and calculated. Instead we should be honest with ourselves and ask the Holy Spirit to rekindle our hearts with fresh fire from the altar.

To pray in the Spirit is to develop a sensitive ear to hear and a willing heart to respond to the urges of the Spirit. We do this as follows:

- Yield to the gentle influences of the dove.
- Plead with him to breathe into us his life, impart into our hearts his concerns, drop a piece of his heart into our hearts and share his pain. Wait for the Spirit to drop things into your spirit.
- By the Holy Spirit assisting us to *identify* with and have compassion for those he loves, so that we can truly sit where the

people sit, weep as they weep and rejoice with those who do rejoice.
- Feel the wind of the Spirit under our wings, and like the eagle, soar high above all danger and obstacles; free from limitations.
- Allow the Holy Spirit to transport us to realms unknown.
- When we reach our extremity, give God opportunity to open new possibilities for us.

Prayer and speaking in tongues

When our words run dry and our vocabulary is inadequate let us employ our new tongues. Speak mysteries in other tongues to the burdens, demons and the thick weighty darkness that surround us. The gift of tongues is a powerful tool at the disposal of every believer to use in worship, prayer and intercession. To pray in the Spirit is to allow the life, love and power of God to flow in you and through you to fill the throne-room of God. It is allowing God to pray his burdens through us.

Praying in the Spirit is to be drawn into increasing intimacy with Christ

King David was a great worshipper and a man of deep intercession. The prayers he prayed and the psalms he wrote bear abundant witness to this fact (1 Chronicles 29:10–15). Here was a man to whom the Holy Spirit gave revelations of the greatness, the power, the majesty and the glory of the Lord. He once said,

> One *thing* I have desired of the LORD, that will I seek; that I may dwell in the house of the LORD all the days of my life, to behold the beauty of the LORD, and to inquire in His temple. For in the time of trouble He shall hide in His pavilion: in the secret place of His tabernacle He shall hide me, He shall set me high upon a rock. (Psalms 27:4–5)

The same is true of Enoch who walked so close with God that he was translated.

Abraham was known to be such a friend of God that the Lord did not withhold anything from him. Moses had personal, intimate encounters with God at the burning bush and at Mount Sinai. Such was the power of the meeting that he was filled with the presence of the Lord and his face shone with divine glory unaccustomed to human eyes. What more can we say of men like Elijah, Daniel, Peter, James and John on the Mount of Transfiguration, Paul who was caught up to the third heaven, and John who was in the Spirit on the Lord's day on Patmos? They were all men of prayer drawn into an intimacy with God that transformed their entire lives. As we consecrate ourselves in prayer, the Holy Spirit will inevitably lead us into his inner chamber where the Shekinah glory dwells; where the brightness of holiness overwhelms and where the awesomeness of his person outshines a million suns: there to behold his beauty. Paul said to the Christians in Galatia that we have received the promised Holy Spirit by faith who will paint, as an artist, clear and beautiful pictures of the Christ (Galatians 3:14, *cf* 1).

To pray with power we need to have fresh revelations of the Christ person so that we can know him more; so that we will always have a tender conscience toward God and increase in our confidence and faith. 'Come Holy Spirit, open our eyes and draw us ever closer until we are overwhelmed by your love and lost in adoration, wonder and praise.' As we linger in his presence may we hear the voice of the Spirit summoning us to come up higher, into the other-worldly realm: a temporary flight from the mundane and ridiculous humdrum of everyday existence to the noble sublime. There we can taste the powers of the age to come (Ephesians 1:18–23; Hebrews 6:5).

Oh Spirit, give us new visions of an omnipotent sovereign God. Affirm our faith in a God who is mightier than the human mind. Dispel our man-made assumptions of God that we have created for ourselves. Destroy the limitations we have invented and give us a fresh understanding of the

God of the New Testament. Restore to us a pre-scientific worldview of a God who works miracles and is actively involved with people in the outworking of his will on earth. As we bow our knees in earnest expectation, Lord, lift up our heads and transport us to realms of pure delight. Fill us with such ecstasy of who the Christ person really is and who we are in him until our hearts are released in spontaneous explosion of unbridled passion, adoration and joy in the Holy Spirit. Until our voices blend with the heavenly hosts to cry 'HOLY, HOLY, HOLY is the Lord of hosts; WORTHY, WORTHY, WORTHY is the Lamb that was slain.'

Praying in the Spirit involves intercession

Intercession is a prophetic and priestly function of the Church. It is the responsibility to stand before God to represent others. It is ability to so identify with others to plead their cause as though it is your own. There is an incarnation aspect to this Holy Spirit-anointed ministry of intercession. It is the willingness to take upon oneself the sins, pain, plight, problems and heartaches of others. But even far more important is to capture what is in God's heart for them and be willing to bear them on his behalf in prayer. In a very real and personal sense it literally means having the attitude that was in Christ Jesus, who, being in the form of God, did not consider it robbery to be equal with God, but made himself of no reputation, taking the form of a servant, and coming in the likeness of men. He emptied himself of his privileges, humbled himself and became obedient to the point of death on the cross (Philippians 2:5–10).

Jesus invites his people to share his high-priestly ministry. We have a great high priest seated at the right hand of God who is touched with every feeling of our weaknesses and lives completely to intercede for us. To be productive in intercession we must be willing to identify with people and their weaknesses. Abraham stood before God and pleaded with him to save Sodom until he ran out of options. He persevered to the utmost (Genesis 18:16–33). Moses returned to the Lord and said, 'Oh, these people have sinned a great sin, and have made for themselves a god of gold! Yet now, if you will forgive their sin – but if not, I pray, blot me out of your book which you have written.' Daniel and Nehemiah in their intercession for the people totally identified with them. The Holy Spirit is the only one appointed and sent to communicate what God sees in people and how much compassion he feels for them. He deposits in our hearts those concerns, then he empowers us to bring them to the throne of grace in fervent prayer.

Intercession is three-dimensional. I come to God for *me*. God ministers to me and at the same time imparts his burdens for others into my heart. I then convey these back to him most times with great intensity, agony, travail and persevering persistence. He in turn reaches out to touch the persons concerned out of his great love and mercy. It is time that the Church becomes pregnant with the deep concerns of Jesus' heart and faithfully carries them in her womb until the conception becomes actual births in the kingdom. The future of many generations is dependent on our willingness to intercede. When Zion travailed she gave birth to her children (Isaiah 66:8).

Praying in the Spirit is invasion of enemy territory

Paul exhorted the Corinthian Church to pray in the Spirit and sing in the Spirit. The Lord has commissioned the Church corporately to exercise authority on earth that governs activity in heaven. 'Whatever you bind on earth will be bound in heaven and whatever you loose on earth will be loosed in heaven' (Matthew 18:18). The Church governs God's action in heaven *now*. What an awesome responsibility! So much of God's redemptive purposes for humanity depend on how effectively the Church discharges this responsibility. The destiny of many generations and nations will be realized when the Church asserts its authority in Christ to free them from the captivity and bondage of Satan's evil works. Surely the execution of this mission of the Church cannot be accomplished without the intervention of the Holy Spirit. In every instance when the Holy Spirit intervened in the affairs of humanity in Acts, prayer preceded it. It seems to suggest that prayer is a prerequisite to revival. The Church can only fulfil its mission when operating under the anointing of the Spirit (Acts 1:8). Even Jesus was anointed by the Spirit to minister (Luke 4:18; Acts 10:38). The Holy Spirit anointing equips and empowers the Church to fulfil the will of God. Through prayer that anointing is released. The oil of anointing breaks every yoke.

Like a mighty army let us arise O church, and march forward into battle to plunder hell to populate heaven. Church, arise: restore a radical and revolutionary understanding of Holy Spirit prayer. I will pray with the spirit and sing with the spirit and sing with the understanding too! (1 Corinthians 14:15).

PRAYING FROM THE UNDERSIDE: BREAKING FORTH INTO LIBERATION

Ronald A. Nathan

Ronald A. Nathan is an international development consultant, community theologian and a lecturer. He was formerly the Director of the African and Caribbean Evangelical Alliance. His previous experiences include pastoral duties in Clapham and Croydon, south London, and as Senior Church Minister in Trinidad and Tobago. He has lectured at Bridgebuilders, London; Central Bible Institute, Birmingham; Wesley College, Bristol; Centre for Black and White Christian Partnership, Birmingham; Lewisham College, London; and Westminster College, Oxford, covering subjects such as Africentricity, Black Theology, Spirituality and Black Mental Health, Culture and Personhood, etc.

He is the writer of numerous articles for the *Voice*, *New Nation* and the *Journal* newspapers. He has written articles for *Black Theology in Britain*, *New International Review of Missions* and *Political Theology*. He has also published contributions in three books.

He has travelled widely in the Americas, Europe and Africa as a motivational speaker, lecturer and preacher. He has visited 25 African countries. He has qualifications in Theology, Cross-cultural Communication, Adult and Further Education. He is a graduate of Oxford University with a Masters' in Applied Theology and at present is a PhD candidate at the University of Birmingham.

With sleepy eyes we stumbled out of our warm beds, summoned to our grandparents' bedside for morning devotions. It was a confusing experience for me and my sisters. I was a child of ten years old, my sisters were eight and six. What could be so important that we had to get out of bed at such an ungodly hour as 5 a.m. each weekday to pray? In later years, I discovered that there was more to pray for than there were hours in the day. This is a personal reflection on 30 years of praying and listening to prayers. It maps out an ever-evolving experience of how prayer becomes a tool of liberation.

I was always a curious and questioning child in church and

outside of it. I would not let any opportunity go by from which I could get answers to some question or the other. I drove my grandmother to despair at times. Prayer was not some mystical exercise to me – it was a rich source of current news and commentary which raised new questions. I deducted, from the prayers I listened to, what was happening in the lives of family, friends, brothers and sisters.

Children in those days were expected to be seen but not heard. They were told very little about what was taking place, even when they were directly affected.

Prayers were central to the Christian's existence, an indispensable component of one's spirituality. I was introduced to a variety of different prayer events. One's own devotional life consisted of personal daily prayer and family prayers. A family experiencing some spiritual oppression could request a cottage meeting. This saw the church paying a visit to your home and praying for deliverance. In my youthful need to see some familiar television programme, I prayed that deliverance would come before my scheduled TV sitcom. These prayer meetings could go on and on and on. Once I lost my bed to the praying brothers, who stayed so late that they could not make their way back to their homes.

There were times when an unsaved (non-Christian or outsider) member of the home would be the special focus of the prayers. Trinidadians understood this phenomenon as 'praying on the person's head'. This is not to be mistaken with the laying-on of hands upon the head of a person in need of prayers of healing.

At the local church we *had* to attend the weekly prayer meeting. There were very few acceptable reasons for not attending. Then there were the special occasions when a week of prayer meetings would be organized. These took place at the beginning of the year, for example, to see the New Year in. At other times they warranted a week's prayer to aid the effectiveness of a special series of evangelistic meetings called 'crusades'.

Then there were the monthly prayer and fasting days. The discipline of fasting went hand-in-hand with praying. It was not easy for some of us, but we tried, as we were committed to seeing miracles take place. There was a time around my sixteenth birthday when there was a 40-day fast. This was indeed an exceptional occasion.

Every other month we would have all-night prayer meetings. These ran from 10 p.m. to 5 a.m. the following day. You can therefore imagine that by the time I was fourteen years old I had heard thousand of prayers which had widened my informal education of community affairs and denominational gossip. The older I got, the more determined I was to listen very attentively to the prayers of others. My attitude changed somewhat when I made a personal commitment to Jesus Christ: in other words, I got 'saved'. I was now an insider. This did not remove my curiosity – it just expanded it. I now became interested in the things that sisters and brothers did not pray for. Prayers in our churches were normally vocal and therefore open for the examination of all 'who had ears to hear'.

I was intrigued, for example, that there were no prayers to God against racism, class exploitation and political nepotism. There were no prayers for help to remain faithful in marriage; even though it was needed, it just was not said. No prayers were uttered for young women who could not find suitable husbands. No prayers stormed the kingdom of God for justice in South Africa. No prayers of deliverance for the oppressed in Caribbean societies and communities to be set free. There were no prayers in opposition to Ronald Reagan's war games in the Caribbean Sea or any fire placed on his head for the slaughter of innocent Grenadians and Cubans during the US invasion of Grenada. This confused me as a child of God wanting to make my faith relevant to the situation I faced in school, at home and on the streets. No prayers were said for the black power activists seeking equality in a world of white supremacy. I was therefore curious as to what made some subjects acceptable as prayer requests and others taboo. I wanted to know; I needed to know; I *had* to know.

The most influential person in my childhood years was my Christian grandmother. Maybe it was due to the fact that I had observed that my grandmother's prayers at home differed from those she prayed at church. At home her exclamations of prayers to God were simple yet profound. She would say, 'Oh Lord lend a hand.' 'Jesus Almighty, give me grace.' 'Look at my crosses.' These prayers were not contrived to impress the other listeners in the prayer meeting – they were straight from the heart.

In case you think I grew up in a monastery on the island of Patmos, let me clarify. I was born in England but was raised by my grandparents in the islands of Trinidad and Tobago. At around the age of ten my grandparents joined the local Pentecostal Church. Prior to that they were Anglicans. Saturated by the church's ethos and its ever-demanding programme, I developed within a separatist subculture which had its own rules and was administered with the austerity of the military. This may be easier to understand given that all of this was happening in a society where churchgoing was a communal ritual.

In such a religious society I heard people praying all around me. There were the Spiritual Baptist's prayers, Catholic's prayers, Anglican's prayers, Seventh-day Adventist's prayers, prayers from criminals and saints, prayers extemporaneous and prayers to be read. I went through the rituals of my own Pentecostal faith and joined the faithful in petitioning God myself. I prayed, prayed with tears, prayed with groaning, prayed in tongues, prayed in the Spirit. However, I was never quite able to shrug off the uncomfortable feeling that there was something not quite right with how I viewed the world. It had to do with how my Christian subculture dealt with people who lived on the underbelly of society. They were the ones who eked out a living on the periphery of our cities and rural communities. Yes, the ones who were seldom consulted, always spoken to and spoken for. They had little or no power to bring about change. They were and are victims of our systems of de-humanization, which allowed the rich to get richer, and the poor to get poorer. Later, I would discover that this was akin to Karl Marx's comment on the possibility of religions becoming 'the opiate of the people'.

One of the first prayers I learnt at my grandparents' bedside altar was the Lord's Prayer. I continued to search for answers to questions too embarrassing to be asked or answered by anyone else but God. In my church tradition these were called special unspoken 'requests'.

God has had to put up with a lot of questioning since those

early days. I was baffled for example by the words from the Lord's Prayer 'Thy Kingdom come, Thy will be done, on earth as it is in heaven . . . thine is the Kingdom, the Power and the Glory.' Did this mean, as I thought it meant, that God is concerned about governance on the earth as in heaven? Yet I was always encouraged to 'seek the things that are above, not the things that are on the earth'. On a number of occasions I was informed, 'You need to sanctify yourself because you approach the Bible with a carnal mind.' Then when the youth leader had had enough of my questioning she said, 'You will get the answers to all your questions in the sweet, sweet bye and bye.'

How pleased I was to read in the book of Psalms prayers that vocalized anger and called for revenge and justice. For as long as I remember I was angry at the state of affairs around me. Why so much poverty? Why so much distress? Why so much suffering? Why did I have to pray in guarded terms about those things that were so prevalent in my society? Why teenage pregnancies? What was God doing all day? Did he not care? There, I had gone and said it, the 'not to be said'. 'One must not interrogate God', I was told.

What was the significance of prayer and its corresponding motivation, faith, if questions for transformation, empowerment and liberation could not be asked? I was learning quickly that I had to be careful who I directed these questions to. Church discipline did not tolerate such 'doubting Thomases'.

Psalm 17 (KJV) was a big hit with me:

Hear the right, O LORD, attend unto my cry, give ear unto my prayer, that goeth not out of feigned lips. (verse 1)

I have called upon thee, for thou wilt hear me, O God: incline thine ear unto me, and hear my speech. (verse 6)

Keep me as the apple of the eye, hide me under the shadow of thy wings. (verse 8)

From the wicked that oppress me, from my deadly enemies, who compass me about. (verse 9)

Now that was the kind of prayer that excited me. It looked life full in the face and said 'I am not having it.' Fundamental to belief in the Christian God is the idea of God as Omnipresent. God was in every situation and knew everything. I lived in dread and fear of displeasing God. So powerful was God that I shrank in horror at approaching 'his throne' about girlfriends and other such trivial matters.

Part of my dread and fear was due to the confused image given to me about God in our church's teachings. There was a right way and a wrong way to pray. There were certain postures that were most conducive to prayer. There were some places especially set aside for prayer. Where in the vicinity I grew up in, could one find a prayer closet, I ask you? It was a miracle if you could find a bed! Who set these parameters?

As I went from Sunday School student to Bible School student, my attitude to prayer changed. Prayer became a professional signature in the race for 'most spiritual' status. The longer I prayed, the more spiritual I was – at least I hoped. Prayer was a rite of passage to saintliness and infallibility. None dared contradict the faithful praying saint. Prayer also became a theological treatise. Of course in a real sense all prayer is theological. I don't deny that. However, I soon learnt the folly of my ways when an elderly saint in my first pastorate shared with me that I was not standing before a theological examination board when I prayed, but was interceding simply for people with needs. These words led me to a liberation of language and expression in prayer.

It was now possible to use Caribbean vernacular in prayer. It was now possible to allow prayer to come from the depths of my culture. These prayers were a reflection of the cultural context of which I was a part. This point has to be understood in light of the colonial history received in the Caribbean and embedded in the formal educational and theological structures.

There are three principles that I have now integrated into my own prayers and prayer life. They do not stand on their own, neither are they exclusive. They just reflect where I am at the moment: they are integrated and do overlap.

First, prayer cannot be dislocated from the social context.

God cannot be isolated from the context in which his children live. The social, economic, political, cultural and spiritual environments within which a people live is essential to their lives. I do not limit prayer solely to the needs of the particular petitioner, church, or denomination. Prayer should be linked to the conditions of the least fortunate in our communities. Prayer should champion the cause of those who are disadvantaged – the sick, the poor – who are invisible in our societies.

Sin is personal and structural, yet it manifests itself in collective ways even as it is seen individually. Therefore prayer becomes a political tool as it works against the oppressive and debilitating circumstances of the people and for their liberation. So let's pray for the homeless, for hurting communities in Liberia and Sierra Leone.

It is at this juncture that I depart from the so-called prosperity preachers who are caught up in themselves, their prosperity, their blessings, their kingdoms and their confessions and to hell with the poor, the sinner, the infirm, unless they buy into their brand of sanitized capitalism. The example of Jesus is significant and sufficient for me as the final arbiter in this matter. Jesus was a friend of publicans and sinners.

Second, prayer cannot be uttered without hope. 'Faith is the substance of things hoped for' we are told by the writer to the Hebrews. Where does hope begin? Hope is not to be entered into after death. It begins with those who are hopeful now! The greatest poverty a people can experience is hopelessness. When our children in schools perceive that it is hopeless to attend school because nothing is expected of them, we must change this perception. The prayers in Sunday School must become more revolutionary.

When young black men are locked away in prison and in a cycle of criminality with little or no chance of reformation, praying people must step in to give them a chance. When unemployment benefits or underemployment are offered to us as a favour for which we must be thankful, we praying people must bring into being industries and jobs of our own. I am committed to working towards the empowerment of the poor, the disenfranchised and the needy. My travels and observations reveal that these are primarily people of colour, black people.

I am of the firm conviction that God is concerned about humankind not as some disembodied personalities called souls but as whole beings needing, among other things, a sense of identity, worth and purpose. This is reflected in my prayers as well as in my other activities.

My prayers have led me to become engaged in building up black communities, that they may be vibrant and powerful. In the face of all forms of insecurity and feelings of inferiority there is need for more religious leaders to commit themselves, and the institutions they lead, to political, cultural, economic and social prayers and actions.

I share with you two prayers I have prayed, which demonstrate my concern for the restoration of respect to African cultures in the African Diaspora. The first is personal, and the second public and communal:

> O God,
> Give me wisdom.
> Wisdom to reclaim the best of the past traditions
> That I may honour and glorify you.
> May I be able to build upon those traditions
> And thereby lift up a standard of greatness for the future.
> Amen!

The next prayer was delivered at the opening of the 1996 African Remembrance Day celebrations.

> O God, Creator and Saviour of all humankind,
>   You are the one to whom we owe our existence from the shores of the Nile.
>   We thank you for allowing us the privilege of gathering today to call upon your blessed name on this day of remembrance.
>   We want to thank you for the opportunity to bring our gifts of the past, our present achievements, and the seeds of the future and to lay them before your feet.

We are assured that there is no sacrificial gift of righteousness and justice that is rejected by you.

So it is with respect and reverence we bring to you the memories of our foreparents. Those who in the face of the most barbaric and wicked institution of criminality called slavery, did not submit to the fears of the unknown or the depths of the blue seas.

Many did not cross the Atlantic but instead crossed over the divide separating the living from the living dead.

We praise you for their tenacity, courage and ingenuity as they refused to endure the restrictions of an enslaved body, a broken spirit and a lost homeland.

We celebrate the lives of those who survived the crossing, chained and harnessed, flogged and flung, ripped off and raped. During hundreds of years of oppression they endured physical, mental, social, cultural, political and spiritual emasculation.

Throughout those centuries you made yourself known, through a spirit that would not surrender. A spirit that ran to the hills and formed communities. A spirit that resisted by running, fighting, sabotaging, organizing and lobbying for freedom.

Thank you for all that they have done to inspire us to step into the unknown of the African Diaspora. Oh God, you are entwined in our past, our present and our future. Give us the strength we need to make a new crossing that will not surrender to police brutality, the slavery of drug abuse, the incarceration of self-inflicted violence and the lies of underachievement.

May the memory of those past Africans reconcile us to our present Africanness. Reconcile us to the best of our traditions and reconcile us to our interdependence.

Yes Lord, this is our prayer, this is our plea, this is our libation, this is our hope, and in these we see our future secured. Amen

The third principle is that prayer cannot be left unescorted. What I mean by this is, just as faith without works is dead, prayer without transforming action is stagnant and repugnant to God. I have always believed, and it has been demonstrated in the ministries I have worked in, that if I pray for a particular need, which is located in a particular context, God calls upon me to be a part of the answer to that prayer, not an observer.

Prayer is not passive: it is resistance of the highest order. It feeds the soul with a robust determination to see things change for the better. It is not satisfied with soundbites of righteousness: it gets involved in radical action.

Prayer for the homeless is intrinsically linked to lobbying for more affordable housing. Prayer for healing is associated with mediation work in communities ripping themselves apart.

At a meeting of a small, black self-help group, I prayed:

Merciful Creator God.

We are indebted to you.

It is beyond our capacity to repay you for all that you have been and done for us, through us, and in us.

We thank you for the strength you have given to us to engage in the struggle against racism, Xenophobia, and other forms of bigotry and injustice.

Please may our eyes be always opened and our spirits closed to any injustice we may commit in our haste to secure justice and to bring in your kingdom.

To you O Lord, be all praise, adoration and respect for the grace that covers us all. Amen.

During the inquiry to the Stephen Lawrence murder, I cried as I prayed at the inertia of the black churches to this calamity.

O God, may the murder of Stephen help us to recognize that our spirituality cannot remain locked away in the halls of our worship.

May we be provoked by this brutal racist act, provoked to be salt and light on the earth.

Give us the determination to fight on every front, ignorance and prejudice that result in such a tragic loss of a young life.

May we be able to redirect our efforts to making this island a home for all peoples regardless of our race, colour or gender.

Give us the courage to agitate, demonstrate, petition and advocate in the face of intimidation and threats, for a new way of relating and living with those who are different from ourselves.

O God if we have to, we are willing to face oppression, beatings, harassment and race crimes in the interest of a better world for the Stephens of today and tomorrow.

May we never resort to the comforts of silence and inactivity as we sing our hymns, dance in the Spirit and collect our offerings. This I pray in your name. Amen.

I resist injustice even when it is couched in religious language and disguised in prayer. Recently I was at a service at which I heard a pastor praying. He was giving thanks to God for the release of the British hostages in Liberia. One may be forgiven for being genuinely impressed by such a trendy minister. He had listened to the BBC news earlier that morning and demonstrated a willingness to be contemporary and relevant to his congregation. Alas, I was shocked and appalled to find that God was revered in thanksgiving for the two white hostages liberated, but no prayer was said for the hundreds of African children kidnapped and held by the same group of rebels. Here the Church was endorsing and baptizing British foreign policy and ignoring the plight of the less fortunate.

Our missionary prayers have to be better informed of global development issues. If without a vision the people perish, how can we be selfish in prayer?

Prayer meetings, prayer convocations, prayer conventions and prayer concerts all require a new dynamism. The least attended meeting of the Christian Church is the prayer meeting. They are boring, irrelevant and archaic in language and practices. Let's put some life into them by going on prayer walks that would lead us to gather outside the National Front offices in South London and call down the wrath of God on the heads of those demented people. Let's bring liberation and freedom by marching on

Downing Street and praying for those who are socially ostracized by our capitalistic systems. Let's urge our church structures to reform themselves into agencies of liberation, hope and empowerment. Let us in our prayer of courage name the drug barons and the drug companies that are poisoning our communities.

Yes, I too want revival and pray for it. We need a revival of spirit, a revival of purpose, a revival of equality, a revival of full employment, a revival of sanity from the madness of drive-by shootings. A revival that would result not only in our churches being full but the prisons being emptied. I pray for a revival that would raise the potential of people of colour. Our people need a revival that would allow them to go wherever their aspirations and potential would lead them.

I acknowledge that we are indeed a spiritual people by nature of the fact that our worldview is consistent with a God that is always in our midst. This fact must not be used just for pietistic utterances but for the salvation of the world. Salvation does not end at the door of the church or sanctification at our denomination's headquarters.

I thank God that prayer has played such a significant part in my life and my spirituality. It has made me conscious of the transcendent. It has saved me from living in despair. It has allowed me to face life-struggles with a balanced sense of my responsibility and a yearning for something better. I am aware of prayer as a cry from the innermost being of a person. This, I know, can bring conflict with our religious institutions and practices.

I have come a long way in evolving a lifestyle that grasps the significance of the Gospel's impact on the lives of people from the underside. It can transform their existence and empower them to live a liberated life. This miracle works when, in partnership and fellowship with God, we establish structures and rituals based on the values of the kingdom of God. These will testify to the scripture's promise that 'who the Son of Man sets free, they are free indeed'. Thank you Lord.

Note

All scriptural quotations are from the King James Version of the Bible.

INTER-GENERATIONAL CONVERSATIONS AND PRAYER

Anthony Reddie

Anthony G. Reddie is a Research Fellow in Christian Education at the Queen's Foundation for Theological Education. This post is a dual one, as he is also a Research Consultant in Christian Education to the Methodist Church. Anthony has a background in Christian youth and children's work, and has written extensively on this area for a number of years. In 1998, his two-volume work *Growing Into Hope*, an African-centred Christian education curriculum was published – the first of its kind in Europe. Anthony successfully completed his doctorate in March 2000 from the University of Birmingham. His thesis was concerned with the Christian Education of African Caribbean children.

Introduction

I have spent the past four and half years engaged in doctoral research in the area of Christian education. My concern was to create a new paradigm for the Christian education and nurture of African Caribbean children in Birmingham. Central to this enterprise was the creation of a newly developed African-centred Christian education that was built upon the liberative principles of black theology.

The development of this curriculum provided the substantive element of my doctoral work. This curriculum was completed in late 1997 and was published the following year by the Methodist Publishing House (Reddie, 1998a).

Following the publication of *Growing into Hope*, my attentions were drawn towards the informal, more oblique forms of Christian education and nurture – Christian education that arises through the medium of the family, the examples of Christian living and discipleship that arise through the family and its interactions with the various constituent members, its dialogue with the past through familial remembering and folk-lore, and the engagement with the present.

The concept of the family in African Caribbean life is hugely important. Particular emphasis must be placed upon those older members who made the long journey from the Caribbean in the post-Second World War migration. These individuals remain the solidifying presence in the ongoing survival of inner-city churches in Britain. According to the early quantitative work at the outset of the research, the majority of African Caribbean children are taken to church by a grandparent (Reddie, 2000). These older individuals remain important for their continued commitment to inner-city churches. Were it not for their tenacity, diligence and strength of faith, these churches would no longer exist. The importance of these individuals was increased following the departure of the white middle class from the inner cities (Reddie, 1999a, pp. 22–3).

One would be hard pressed to deny the importance of retentive African cultures emanating from the Caribbean for connoting identity and self-concept among African Caribbean children and young people. One need only consider the continuing popularity of a whole host of musical forms and idioms emanating from the Caribbean, to appreciate the resonance of that region upon the consciousness of present-day African Caribbean youth.

The importance of these older African Caribbean people lies in the direct link between these individuals and the Caribbean. The greater majority of them were born in the Caribbean. The experiences, family narratives and stories of faith are potentially vital resources for enabling African Caribbean children to discover aspects of their otherness. Hazareesingh offers a useful methodology for enabling young children to elicit familial narratives from their parents. Additionally, she posits a useful rationale for these forms of familial remembering (Hazareesingh, 1994, pp. 27–9).

In order to supplement the earlier curriculum-driven attempts at creating a new paradigm for the Christian education of African Caribbean children and young, I felt it necessary that I explore more oral-based approaches to the teaching and learning of the Christian faith. This alternative approach would be located within a number of African Caribbean families, and facilitated by a series of intergenerational conversations between older and younger members of the family.

My contacts with a number of older African Caribbean men and women in these inner-city churches had alerted me to the important element of narrative and folk-tales in the lives of these individuals. An important moment in the genesis of this, the final phase of the research project, occurred when I was invited to speak to a fellowship group in one of the participating churches.

I attempted to engage with these women and men in order to assist them in supporting and encouraging their grandchildren in the Christian faith. The resulting session was to have a profound influence upon my subsequent thinking and action.

As these women and men informed me about their experiences of growing up in the Caribbean, I began to gain a clearer understanding into how these varied contexts had shaped both their experience and their expressions of faith. Many of these people had a secure and grounded sense of their own identity. In stark contrast to their grandchildren, they remembered, with great vividness, being nurtured in secure environments where they experienced an acute sense of belonging. Many of them spoke of the church, and their role and participation within that setting, as being one where they felt truly affirmed.

I had gained a sense of the dynamics of this facet of African Caribbean experience by means of this discourse with older African Caribbean members of this inner-city church. I hoped, through the course of these conversations, to assess the viability of African Caribbean elders sharing aspects of their faith and experiences with younger members of the family. What would emerge from these conversations? How would they impact upon the consciousness of younger African Caribbean children and young people?

In conceptual terms, I perceived this final phase of the project as an attempt to develop an alternative perspective on Christian education in inner-city historic–mainline churches. If the creation and implementation of *Growing into Hope* represented the visible, public forms in which Christian education is practised within the Church, then the oral tradition posits an alternative perspective. The oral tradition is the informal, often invisible means of nurturing and educating children and young people in faith. This alternative facility arises when guardians share stories of experience and familial narratives with succeeding generations. I wanted to find a means of developing this area, which one might describe as the flip-side of the Christian education coin.

Over the next fifteen months, I approached a number of families and constructed a mechanism by which a series of structured conversations might take place between African Caribbean people of differing ages and contexts. A number of fascinating elements arose from these structured familial discussions, and in this chapter I will relay my impressions and reflections from one particular discussion with an African Caribbean family belonging to an inner-city Methodist church in Birmingham. This extended family consisted of the grandmother, who was in her seventies and had arrived from Jamaica in 1960; she had two daughters, one in her late forties, the other in her late thirties. The older daughter was accompanied by her own daughter, who was sixteen years old at the time of our conversation.

As this research relates to the Christian education of African Caribbean children and young people, I am interested primarily in the educational possibilities of this area of African Caribbean life. What therefore are the elements that might assist African Caribbean children in their affective development? First, I would like to highlight an important theme that resonated throughout the course of these inter-generational conversations.

The importance of prayer

Prayer was an important resource for all the members of this family. It should be noted, however, that the fluency and the literal appropriation of God's answers to prayer differed markedly between the grandmother and the granddaughter. Whereas the grandmother prayed at all times for strength and discernment, the granddaughter's own prayers were largely relegated to her final moments before sleep. The granddaughter perceived herself as having less faith than her mother. The granddaughter came to this conclusion by making reference to the christening of a niece. Her mother's ability to instantly pray for a child, asking God's blessing upon her niece, was somehow in stark contrast to the granddaughter's own perceived lack of dexterity in the area of extempore prayer.

I will not attempt to make generalizations on either the extent or the quality of African Caribbean theological reflection. This aspect of the research was far too limited in scope, and of a highly qualitative nature for that form of universal analysis and potential application. From this limited data, however, one can make a number of informed hypotheses about the nature of the oral tradition between different generations of African Caribbean people.

The world from which the grandmother and daughter gained their formative influences is one that is highly religious and less plural than the current British context. The Caribbean of the 1950s and 1960s was passing through a colonial, pre-independence epoch of extreme poverty and struggle (Williams, 1970; Randle, 1993; Hall, 1981). For the greater majority of people living in the diverse islands of the Caribbean, amelioration from concrete realities of poverty and marginalization emanated from the Church. This identification with the Christian faith as a means of liberating praxis has an historic dimension. The grandmother and the elder daughter's literal appropriation of prayer as a means of overcoming contextual struggles find echoes in the actions and beliefs of slaves on the Caribbean islands.

Kortright Davis asserts that slaves never accepted a transcendent construct of God that was remote and above the sufferings of black people. Conversely, the slaves held on to a concept of an immanent God that was alongside them in their struggles (Davis, 1990, p. 59). Davis reminds us that African people believe strongly in the immediacy of supernatural beings that exist alongside ordinary human beings in their common existence (Davis, 1990).

Grandmother's religious upbringing has been influenced by

syncretic African beliefs, which are expressed in an overtly literal, immanentist approach to Christianity. These influences may have given her a particular approach to her faith that is significantly different from that within her granddaughter's experience. It is not my intention to make any qualitative judgements concerning the respective faith and expressions of faith of the various members of this family.

My belief is that the granddaughter's expressions of faith have been influenced by the less pietistic milieu into which she has been socialized. The multiracial, highly pluralistic context in which the granddaughter has gained her formative experiences is very different from the world of her immediate forebears.

There are stark differences between the formative experiences of the granddaughter and her older relatives. Can one reasonably expect a white-dominated, Western society to be a sympathetic setting in which traditional notions of one's African identity are expressed? An identity that has been forged in the particularity of the Caribbean and influenced by a syncretic past from the continent of Africa cannot exist in the British context without being subject to change.

The granddaughter's self-understanding, and her notions of faith, lack the rhetorical flourish of her grandmother. I do not contend that the granddaughter should strive to replicate the discourse of her immediate forebears. There are benefits from the granddaughter having access to the religio-cultural experiences of her mother and grandmother, particularly in the shaping of her own identity and sense of belonging (Westerhoff III, 1976). Replication and mirroring remain an unrealistic goal, and are not the primary aims of this piece of action–reflection research. Moreover, the realities of this particular context cannot be understood simply through a restating of the past.

The educational possibilities of this area of work lie in the potentialities they provide for the effective development of African Caribbean children. Michael Clarke states that one of the primary difficulties facing young black people in their maturation and development is the discontinuity that exists between them and their past. He writes: 'I have noted that in our developing, technological society there has been a significant shift from the past, especially in the transmission of faith. No longer are the elderly the transmitters of stories; in fact there is little dialogue between the youth and the aged' (Clarke, 1995, p. 4).

Clarke asserts that the fragmentary nature of contemporary urban life has led to an all too apparent divergence in diasporan African Caribbean life. This is manifested in the discontinuity between African peoples of differing generations. Clarke continues by stating that 'We must discover ways to pass on our stories, stories that tell us who we are, stories that will help individuals to continually discover God's presence in their lives' (Clarke, 1995, p. 4).

By exposing African Caribbean children to the narratives and expressions of faith of their forebears, these individuals gain access to survival strategies and aphoristic wisdom that might assist them in their existential struggles. The latter part of our group discussion provided opportunities for family members to offer a brief intimation of their sense of hope for the future. In this portion of the discussion, it became clear that the granddaughter's own hopes for the future were buoyed by the very real support and affirmation she had gained and continued to receive from older members of her family.

The importance of prayer as a concrete resource for surmounting struggle and achieving liberation resonates very firmly within the diasporan African experience. From the time of slavery through to the present day, the facility of prayer has given substance and cohesion to the liberation impulse within the exilic experience of diasporan Africans. For black women, prayer has been the means of instilling hope in their children (Carter, 1984, pp. 80–109).

The discourse of this inter-generational session provided me with an opportunity to gain a sense of the educational opportunities that might accrue from this non-text-based approach to Christian education. It is instructive to note that when I asked the daughter for comparisons between her own faith and that of her mother, she felt it was difficult to arrive at accurate conclusions. Aside from the qualitative judgements called for in such comparative analysis, the daughter said that 'We haven't really sat down and discussed our faith as such . . . I don't know. We haven't discussed it.'

The lack of formal discussion about matters of faith and stories should not surprise us. The differentiated nature of modern life and the fragmented, even isolated experience of family that affects many individuals, has led to myriad patterns of familial existence (Wimberly, 1999, p. 17). Even a family as close as this one meets in its entirety only one day a week, on a Sunday. There are many families for whom even this limited opportunity for a corporate sense of oneness is not possible.

Within many African Caribbean families in Britain there are many issues related to the ongoing struggles for familial cohesion and a sense of corporate identity. We should not forget some of the current realities at play in present-day Britain. This is a context where lives are governed by the all-pervasive influence of post-modernism. The old assumptions surrounding family life are rapidly disappearing. In this particular epoch the realities of social and geographical mobility are constantly challenging the traditional notions of family cohesion. In light of the aforementioned factors, the opportunities afforded this family through structured conversations were of great importance.

This particular approach was developed as a praxis piece of work, building upon the literature and the previous developments in *Growing Into Hope*. This method enabled this family to engage in a focused type of discourse, which may not have taken place were it not for the intervention of this research project. It is my belief that these forms of inter-generational conversations, while they may possess an element of contrivance, nevertheless perform an important function. This form of structured discourse facilitates the preservation of familial narratives, and historical and socio-cultural experiences. Fred Lofton amplifies the importance of retaining the collective and corporate experiences of African people when he writes: 'Each family must pass on to the next generation the family tree, the heritage, the traditions, and the causes for celebration. The Black family has a special mandate to do so because of past injustices and the failure to preserve much of our group culture' (Lofton, 1991, p. 129).

Reflections on structured conversations

My interactions with this family and a number of other familial groups were to prove very instructive. Prayer remained an important component of the inter-generational discourse of these families. In ways that were remarkably similar to the first family, younger members of other families were taught to pray by their older relatives. In a number of the accounts, the traditional prayer of 'Gentle Jesus' seemed to represent some form of signifier in connoting aspects of an African Caribbean religio–cultural heritage. This prayer was an important moment in my own sense of identity in religio–cultural terms. I have distinct memories of being taught this prayer at my mother's knee (something of a cliché I know, but nonetheless absolutely true) at a very young age.[1]

God, who in psychological terms may be described as the 'Ultimate Reality' (Fowler, 1981), in this particular understanding of prayer, is identified in immanent terms. God, through the life, death and resurrection of Jesus, and by and through the power of the Holy Spirit, is manifested in God's own creation, mediating alongside humankind, who are created in the image of God.

Reference to the importance of a literal, immanentist approach to prayer has been highlighted in a previous publication (Reddie, 1999b, p. 72). My mother, in particular, inculcated the importance of praying to God at all times. Accompanying this approach to prayer was the literal, almost eager expectation that God would answer one's petition. There was never any doubt within my mother's conceptualization of God, that God was not in the business of assisting and supporting the presence of God's own people. The faithful would be upheld and no forces would overpower them. In this respect, the words of Romans 8:37–39 ring true. The author of this text writes:

> In everything we have won more than a victory because of Christ who loves us. I am sure that nothing can separate us from God's love – not life or death, not angels or spirits, not the present or the future, and not powers above or powers

below. Nothing in all creation can separate us from God's love for us in Christ Jesus our Lord! (*The Contemporary English (Version) Bible*, 1995, p. 1363)

Whilst it would be disingenuous of me to imply that I remain wedded to the theology and the practice of my mother's approach at the time of writing, it would be true to remark that a good deal of my present understanding of prayer owes much to the philosophy inculcated into me during my formative years. My theology has developed and changed over the years,[2] absorbing a multitude of influences that have affected both the form and the content of my faith.[3] Yet, at the centre of my theological reflections, at the very heart of my spirituality and awareness of the presence of God, lie many of the maxims taught me by my mother.

The importance of inter-generational conversations, particularly as they relate to the facility of prayer, cannot be overstated. As a pedagogical tool, the methodology of sharing conversations between different generations has much to commend it. In the Christian nurture and socialization of black children and young people, perhaps we have been guilty of relying too exclusively upon formalized, textual approaches to the task of creating new generations of believers. Colleen Birchett reminds us that formalized, textual approaches to the teaching and learning process of Christianity (particularly the area of prayer) are quite recent innovations (Birchett, n.d., pp. 74–82). Ella P. Mitchell, conversely, stresses the importance of informal, inter-generational communication between people of African descent (Mitchell, 1986, pp. 92–101). Mitchell draws upon the experiences of African Americans during the epoch of slavery, to highlight the importance of African elders passing on their experiences and narratives to succeeding generations (1986, p. 92). Romney Moseley stresses the importance of inter-generational communication, particularly within the context of the Black Church when he writes, 'Reconnecting black youth to their ancestral heritage and transmitting intergenerational faith is the responsibility of the black church' (Moseley, 1989, p. 89).

My commitment to both the methodology of oral-based,

inter-generational conversations between African Caribbean elders and their grandchildren, is informed by my practice as a Christian educator and practical theologian. Within the context of my research, I wanted to find a means of encouraging older black people to share insights of their experiences and narratives with younger family members. This commitment to oral-based approaches to education and nurture is not intended to negate the central, almost pivotal importance of writing and text-based approaches to theology and Christian formation.

The initial thrust of my research was directed within the observable and tangible domain of curriculum development. This focus of the research is manifested in the two volumes of Christian education material that emerged from this academic inquiry (Reddie, 1998a). These books are the first of their kind in Europe, and I am pleased that they have emerged from within the experiences of a black researcher, working collaboratively with black young people and children. Whether one agrees with them or not, these publications are authentic expressions of black, African Caribbean selfhood and Christian reflection in Britain. It remains crucial that people of African descent are at the forefront of detailing and describing their experiences in print, be it within academic journals or through the medium of popular literature. As the editor of this book has often reminded me, 'If we don't write our stories, then others will do it for us.' I think this dictum remains a powerful reminder that we have to be the custodians of our own experiences. As my elders have often remarked, 'He (or she) who feels it, knows it.'

Despite the important claims for writing, I feel there remains an ongoing importance, however, for oral approaches to Christian education and nurture. This importance lies in two areas – within the context of prayer (the central concern of this essay) and the methodology of oral, inter-generational conversations, as the receptacle for this Christian, spiritual form of empowerment.

With reference to these twin areas, I shall deal with the methodological point first, looking briefly at the importance of the form in which notions of prayer are communicated from one generation to the next. Ella P. Mitchell reminds us of the importance of formative, relational models of Christian education and nurture which arise through the interaction of children and young people and their forebears. Mitchell states that, for the greater majority of black Christians, the nurturing of their Christian faith and the various components of that faith (especially that of prayer) has been 'caught, not taught' (Mitchell, 1986, p. 111).

Despite the claims of text-based approaches to Christian education, nurture and formation, and the very real inherent problems that preclude oral approaches to the educative and socialization tasks, there can be no real substitute for the role of personal example. Reflecting upon my own experiences, I have learnt what it is to be a Christian from my parents (Reddie, 1999b; Reddie, 1998b, pp. 53–60). No amount of prescribed, planned, curriculum-driven teaching (no matter how worthy and important these approaches remain) could compensate for the presence of committed and responsible elders who both practised and demonstrated the importance of prayer by their daily observance of this rite of Christian experience and discipleship.

I am well aware of the many associated difficulties and assumptions implicit in this form of education. What if the parents and the immediate significant others are not practising Christians? From whom will the child learn about the importance of prayer? Within the Methodist tradition, I know that we have lost one, if not two, generations of African Caribbean adults. The greater majority of black children attend church (if they attend church at all) without the active presence of a parent.

Whilst this ongoing situation is undoubtedly a cause for concern, an additional factor alerts us to the possibilities and opportunities for Christian education and nurture, particularly as they relate to prayer. My research in Birmingham (Reddie, 2000) has highlighted the fact that the greater numbers of African Caribbean children[4] attend church with a grandparent. These older African Caribbean elders, often termed the 'Windrush Generation' have become the stalwarts of many inner-city congregations, whether within the 'mainstream' or 'black-led' traditions (Reddie, 1999a).

I believe it is these individuals who provide the essential link between the historic appropriation of the facility and the power of prayer, which has sustained countless generations of black people of the African Diaspora, and younger generations born and socialized in this country. The example of lived experience and prayerful dedication and discipleship can provide models by which black children and young people can begin to gain some semblance of the factors, both immanent and transcendent, that have enabled people of African descent to survive the many travails of the past. Janice Hale says something to this effect when reflecting upon the importance of re-telling stories of experience, by word and example. She writes, 'These stories transmit the message to Black children that there is a great deal of quicksand and the many land mines on the road to becoming a Black achiever . . . They also transmit the message that it is possible to overcome these obstacles' (Hale, 1995, p. 207).

If the form in which the facility of prayer can be shared between differing generations of black people is of crucial import, then the substantive elements of prayer remain even more so. In an epoch of tremendous technological and social change, when the age-old traditions of pre-modernity and modernity are fast disappearing, there can be a tendency for educationalists to seek recourse to new techniques and disciplines as possible avenues for engaging with the ferment of the present age. Developmental psychologists, sociologists, cultural and literary theorists and ethnographers are busily engaged in the process of positing hypotheses for the myriad malaise that has seemingly enveloped the present zeitgeist.

An important resource that can assist our children and young people in the post-modern playground (Roebben, 1997, pp. 332–47) of choice, nihilism and confusion that seemingly pervade the air, is the facility of prayer. Not the kind of prayer which dulls the sensibilities to the realities of pain and struggle that is evidenced all around us. Not the kind of prayer that seeks refuge in certain forms of abstractions that describe a personal piety, which retreats from the world as it is, in all its worst manifestations. Not the kind of prayer that denies solidarity with others who are struggling from the multiple forms of oppression that plague this world.

The kind of prayer of which I speak is the facility that connects with the very heart of God. Prayer that demands reflective action. The kind of prayer that is an integral component of faith, whose practical, demonstrable consequences are described in James 2:14–26. The demand for praxis (action and reflection) finds expression in the salient words of Paulo Freire who opined that 'Action without reflection is mere activism, and reflection without action is pure verbalism' (Freire, 1972, p. 68).

The search for and location of appropriate strategies for surviving and thriving within a racially oppressive, seemingly secular, post-Christian society cannot be anchored upon solely rationalistic, cognitive processes. The search for wholeness and holistic living has been influenced by important discoveries within developmental psychology, emancipatory theologies and transformative education; there remains, however, the crucial import of the transcendent – the numinous power of God. The aforementioned approaches and disciplines should include the latter, but there can be a tendency to forget that our journey of faith is essentially a God-centred pilgrimage that is governed by grace and redemption. There must be the realization that God is beyond the finite limits of our cognition. Yet that same God enters into our struggles and travails, in order that we might experience life in all its fullness.

At its very worst, this Christian polemic of faith adopts all the worst features of self-conscious, learnt religiosity, and vacuous rhetoric. It is the rhetoric of affiliative faith (*Unfinished Business*, 1995, p. 34; Westerhoff III, 1976) – a hand-me-down, imitative faith that is neither grounded in the contextual realities of the 'here and now', nor anchored on an individual connection with the divine, through a personal relationship with Jesus.

Oral-based approaches to Christian education and nurture, particularly the teaching and learning of the resource of prayer, remain important elements in the ongoing narratives of African Caribbean people in Britain. The structure of inter-generational conversations offers an important framework in which the importance and relevance of prayer as a form of liberatory praxis can be expressed. This method and form of Christian education and nurture is not posited as being superior to or possessing greater veracity than text-based approaches to the teaching and learning process. Instead, it is offered as a supplement to systematic, curricula forms of Christian education. The method of oral, inter-generational work seeks to harness the incarnational and relational dynamism of narrative, witness, testimony and example to the ongoing power of transformation that is the Christian Gospel. For African Caribbean elders, transmitting the importance and the powerful reality of prayer is a hugely significant task. It is a task in which the Church has a vital role to play in supporting and encouraging such individuals. The future is *now*, and the importance of prayer in the ongoing life experiences of African Caribbean people remains as vital as ever.

Notes

1 This event and memory of it remains hugely significant in my Christian development. From my mother, I have learnt the importance of prayer and the need to see this as a literal resource in my Christian discipleship.
2 Romney Moseley argues that Christian maturity is achieved through a psychological process of uncoupling the self from certitude and risking all for Christ, through embracing dialogue, mutuality and solidarity with others. Moseley, Romney M., *Becoming A Self Before God* (1991) (Nashville, Tenn.: Abingdon Press) pp. 101–6.
3 See Fowler, James, *Trajectories of Faith: Five Life Stories* (1980) (Nashville, Tenn.: Abingdon Press) for a useful discussion on how context and narrative can influence both the 'How?' and the 'What?' of faith. See also Goldberg, Michael, *Theology and Narrative: A Critical Introduction Stories* (1982) (Nashville, Tenn.: Abingdon Press).
4 Within 'Mainline' or 'Mainstream' churches.

References

Birchett, Colleen (n.d.) 'A history of religious education in the black church', in D. B. Rogers (ed.), *Urban Church Education*, Birmingham, Alabama: Religious Education Press.
Carter, Harold A. (1984) *The Prayer Tradition of Black People*, Baltimore: Gateway Press.
Clarke, David (1995) 'Reclaiming the Black Experience in the Anglican

Church of Barbados: A Study Among a Group of Young Anglicans', unpublished D. Min. thesis, Trinity College, Ontario, Canada.

Davis, Kortright (1990) *Emancipation Still Comin'*, New York: Orbis Books.

Fowler, James (1981) *Stages of Faith*, San Francisco: HarperCollins.

Freire, Paulo (1972) *Pedagogy of the Oppressed*, New York: Herder and Herder.

Hale, Janice (1995) 'The transmission of faith to young African American children', in R. C. Bailey and J. Grant (eds), *The Recovery of Black Presence*, Nashville, Tenn.: Abingdon Press.

Hall, Douglas (1981) *Free Jamaica: 1838–1865: An Economic History*, Aylesbury: Ginn.

Hazareesingh, Sandip (1994) 'Remembering the past: personal memories and family narratives', in S. Hazareesingh, P. Kenway and K. Simms (eds), *Speaking About the Past*, Stoke-On-Trent: Trentham Books.

Lofton, Fred, (1991) 'Teaching Christian values within the family', in Lee N. June (ed.), *The Black Family: Past, Present and Future*, Grand Rapids, Michigan: Zondervan.

Mitchell, Ella P. (1986) 'Oral tradition: the legacy of faith for the black church', in *Religious Education*, Vol. 81, No. 1., Winter.

Moseley, Romney M. (1989) 'Retrieving intergenerational and intercultural faith', in C. R. Foster and G. S. Shockley (eds), *Working with Black Youth*, Nashville, Tenn.: Abingdon Press.

Randle, Ian (1993) *Caribbean Freedom: Society and Economy from Emancipation to the Present*, London: James Currey.

Reddie, Anthony G. (1998a) *Growing Into Hope: Christian Education in Multi-ethnic Churches*, Peterborough: Methodist Publishing House. Volume 1 is entitled *Believing and Expecting*. Volume 2 is *Liberation and Change*.

Reddie, Anthony G. (1998b) 'An unbroken thread of experience', in J. King (ed.), *Family and All That Stuff*, Birmingham: National Christian Education Council.

Reddie, Anthony G. (1999a) 'The journey of a lifetime', in *Magnet: Spellbound*, No. 45, Spring, London: Network, The Methodist Church.

Reddie, Anthony G. (1999b) 'Jesus in the spaces in my life', in R. Harvey (ed.), *Wrestling and Resting: Exploring Stories of Spirituality from Britain and Ireland*, London: CTBI.

Reddie, Anthony G. (2000) 'The Christian education of African Caribbean children in Birmingham: Creating a new paradigm through developing better praxis', Doctoral thesis, Birmingham: Department of Education, The University of Birmingham.

Roebben, Bert (1997) 'Shaping a playground for transcendence: postmodern youth ministry as a radical challenge', in *Religious Education*, Vol. 92, No. 3, Summer.

The Contemporary English (Version) Bible (1995) Nashville, Tenn.: Thomas Nelson.

Unfinished Business: Children in the Churches (1995) London: The Consultative Group on Ministry among Children, CCBI publications.

Westerhoff III, John (1976) *Will Our Children Have Faith?*, New York: Seabury Press.

Williams, Eric (1970) *From Columbus to Castro: The History of the Caribbean – 1492–1969*, London: Andre Deutsch.

Wimberly, Edward P. (1999) *Moving From Shame to Self-Worth: Preaching and Pastoral Care*, Nashville, Tenn.: Abingdon Press.

AFFIRMING GOD'S SOVEREIGNTY IN COPING WITH NATURAL DISASTER: A MONTSERRAT EXPERIENCE

Clarice Barnes and Ruthlyn Bradshaw

Dr Clarice Barnes is a native of Trials, Montserrat. She is an educator and counsellor who has worked throughout the English-speaking Caribbean. Her work includes disaster research and interventions specific to hurricanes and the Montserrat volcanic eruption.

Reverend Ruthlyn Bradshaw is from Hope, Montserrat. She is Pastor of the Dalston New Life Assembly whose congregation consists mainly of Montserratians who have relocated to London as a result of the volcanic eruption.

Montserrat is a 40-square-mile British dependent territory in the Leeward islands of the Caribbean. The pre-eruption population was approximately 12,000 and is currently 5,000. More than half of the relocated population resides in the UK.

Dr Barnes and Reverend Bradshaw have worked jointly in addressing the psycho-social affects of the volcanic disaster through Street and Shelter counselling that incorporates the Montserratian belief in the power of prayer.

Introduction

Natural disasters are a constant part of human experience. Explicit media reports highlight the devastation, loss, displacement, resilience and suffering resulting from such events. The floods of Mozambique, cyclones in India, hurricanes and volcanic eruptions in the Caribbean are but a few high-profiled examples. Natural disasters are often referred to as acts of God, although increasingly there is a view that human beings are partially responsible for such events. Writers such as Anderson (1994) and Walker (1994) point out that the causes and severity of disasters are linked to discrepancies in the allocation and consumption of natural and economic resources. George (1992) argues forcibly that the over-consumption of resources by rich countries in the North holds negative environmental and development consequences for poor countries in the South. For instance, popular commentaries on the Venezuelan floods (December, 1999) and Mozambique (February, 2000) suggest a possible link between deforestation, climatic changes due to global warming and these catastrophes. The fact that natural disasters are generally more prevalent in the South adds more credence to this view.

Whatever the causes, it is well established that natural disasters result in negative human consequences. However, most of the documentation and disaster research are of events in the North where resources are more readily available (Lima and Pai, 1993; Lima *et al.*, 1993). Comparatively less is written about the psycho-social effects for people in the South where natural catastrophes are more frequent. Information on the way people in these localities cope is also sparse. However, Anderson and Woodrow (1989) inform us that poor communities with strong religious beliefs are more able to cope with the psycho-social effects of catastrophe. Moreover, Chemtob (1996), Shelby and Tredinnick (1996) and Pennebaker (1990) alert us to the fact that this is true of people generally. Indeed Barnes' (2000) account of the way Montserratians are coping with their volcanic disaster indicates that there is an abundance of God-talk, particularly statements confirming the power of prayer in dealing with catastrophe.

Montserratians commonly believe that God has ultimate control over the catastrophe and their lives in relationship to it. Consequently many people, particularly the older ones, resist psycho-social interventions that emphasize the healing power of talking through disaster experience with peers or with a professional in favour of speaking directly to God. This is interesting because the distresses of a disaster provide much to talk about, and research on the ways people cope with disaster indicates that they tend to benefit psychologically from retelling the story to interested listeners (Pennebaker, 1990). However, people who experience catastrophe tend to lose interest in listening to the regurgitation of stories of disaster, loss and distress beyond a certain time (Pennebaker and Harber, 1993). Additionally, counselling theorists such as Jackins (1978, 1982) point out that good listeners, that is those who can listen lovingly, non-judgementally without interruption, are not easily found. According to the psalmist, God is the only guaranteed source of such listening, for: 'God has surely listened and heard my voice in prayer. Praise be to God who has not rejected my prayer or withheld his love from me!' (Psalm 66:19–20, NIV).

This chapter discusses the use of prayer in coping with the prolonged and violent upheavals of the Montserrat volcanic eruption. The Montserrat volcanic disaster began in July 1995 when the Soufriere Hills volcano, believed to be dormant for 400 years, erupted. Since then, Montserratians have witnessed, among other things, the destruction of more than three-quarters of the island, the dispersal of most of its 12,000 population overseas, and the cramming of the remainder into the designated safe one-third of the island. The discussion is based firstly on the experiences of the Bethany Pentecostal Church community which engaged in three months of daily, early-morning prayers and affirmations eighteen months into the disaster. Bethany is located within a three-quarter-mile radius of the volcano in the southern part of the island which is now declared an exclusion zone. The majority of its members used to live and work within the same radius. Both authors are members of Bethany, one being its Pastor. Secondly, the discussion is based on an account of a woman who was trapped in the incinerating path of a pyroclastic surge. A pyroclastic flow is a combination of intensely hot ash, gases and rocks that rapidly billow down the flanks of an erupting volcano, and its surge emits the heat of a blast furnace.

The power of prayer in coping with natural disaster

The early-morning prayer fellowship was initiated at Bethany following the return of its members from a month-long evacuation in December 1995 when the volcanic activity heightened, threatening the continuance of life in the southern part of

Montserrat which was home to the majority. Thus we came to the prayer meetings with a combination of experiences of displacement, issues arising from over-crowded shelter living or residence in the homes of friends and family, plus the terrifying spectacle of a growing, glowing volcanic dome. Additionally, we harboured concerns about the risk to health from ash falls and the economic hardships created by the evacuation of households. Out of this context the Bethany community gathered daily (at 5 a.m.) with the belief that God hears and answers prayers. Moreover, we believed strongly that God is greater than the volcano and therefore had it under control. Despite this strongly held assurance, the eruption continued with all of its terror and discomforts. Members reported the feelings of terror that confronted them as they journeyed to church under the threat of the unavoidable glare of the growing fiery dome. Some admitted that, despite their affirmed faith in God's power to protect them, they secretly wondered whether God was in the midst of these experiences. One view was that 'God seems silent and our prayers seem to mock us.'

Nevertheless we continued to pray, asserting that there is no other option, for it is to God alone that we can turn. 'O thou that hearest prayer, unto thee shall all flesh come' (Psalm 65:2, KJV), substantiates this. However, recognizing that it is human to doubt, and that living in an atmosphere of chronic uncertainty is faith-shaking, each prayer meeting ended with an affirmation created from the scripture reading. The affirmation was designed to help us cope with the events of the day. For example, on 3 April 1996 the reading was from Psalm 29:10 (KJV) which declares that 'The Lord sitteth upon the flood.' Out of this statement of the sovereignty of God the affirmation was that: 'Nothing will come my way today that God does not have under control.'

Having made this powerful affirmation, we dispersed at about 6.15 a.m. Four hours later the mountain exploded, emitting the first pyroclastic flow which came dangerously close to the village of Long Ground on the eastern flank of the volcano. Consequently, the entire southern and eastern portions of the island were evacuated – the people never to return.

Those who affirmed the sovereignty of God that morning were faced with homelessness and displacement by the end of the day. Again, there were some who admitted that, although they had earlier affirmed belief in God's power and control as a means of dealing with all that might confront them on that day, they secretly wondered why God allowed the upheaval to happen. Others said that although they did not know exactly how things were going to turn out, they found solace in believing that God had everything under control. The events of the day illustrated this point of faith, for, despite the dangerous nature of the eruption, no lives were lost. Interestingly the event caught the seismologists and the government of Montserrat by surprise, they having predicted only minor rock falls for that day.

Within a day or two we re-grouped on the pastor's veranda, which was by then extended into a church building, using a piece of canvas. The pastor lived in the village of Hope, which was at that time a designated safe area. Within this safe space we spoke of the way God answered our prayers by sparing our lives, providing shelter, and giving us the strength to make a new start. Thus praise and thanksgiving were the focus of these first meetings at Hope. The major portion of this praise was in recognition of the power of prayer and that such power exists even when we momentarily question the speed and actions of God; for God had removed the population of the southern and eastern parts of Montserrat to safety despite the inability of the scientists and the government to predict the impending danger. We might not have regarded our upheaval as an answer to prayer, because most of us had asked God to stop the eruption and protect our homes. Instead, our prayers revealed that God works in mysterious ways. Thus the power of prayer in disaster, as in any situation, lies in our absolute belief in the sovereignty of God. Such a belief is dramatically expressed by Daisy, a resident of Harris, a village on the eastern flank of the volcano. Daisy's account of being trapped within the throes of incineration from a pyroclastic surge further confirms the power of prayer as a means of coping with catastrophe. Her experience illustrates the fact that God provides simultaneous answers to prayer when our needs are desperate.

On that day, the 25 June 1997, I was washing some clothes. I had already washed them and was rinsing them when a young man called Charles tell me to look and see the volcano blow. Well I stop the washing and run. I ran to a little shelter and all the surging came up there. It was very hot and fire was pitching on the electrical cabling. Very, very, hot! And Charles was there. It was like going into an oven heat! That same surge came from the pyroclastic flow that went through mosquito ghaut and people got killed . . . It was not easy and I was there and I called on the name of the Lord. I called on Jehovah, Jehovah help me! I needed help so I called on the Lord and I said, help me please! I called on Jehovah hard you know and he heard my prayer. I prayed and God is so good to me that he spared my life. I did not know that people were down there burn up and cover up until I went down as far as Farms. People get burn up and the place sink. Big house with concrete wall sink! (*sic*).

Daisy's experience shows us that praying is about calling out to God in absolute faith that we would be heard. Moreover, a crisis creates opportunity for unreserved and passionate dependence upon the power and goodness of God. In so doing we cope by personalizing our relationship with God to the extent of understanding that we are made in God's likeness, therefore we possess the power to cope with all things. It is this ability to tap into God's power through prayer that causes many Montserratians who have faced death and irreplaceable loss to continue to affirm the simple truth recognized by Job in his tribulations that 'The LORD gave and the LORD hath taken away' (Job 1:21, KJV).

Conclusion

Natural disaster experiences challenge us to understand and acknowledge the sovereignty of God. However, experiences of extreme loss and threat to survival can create doubt as to whether God is in control, or if he hears our prayers. The most difficult aspects seem to be connected with waiting for our prayers to be answered and in discerning the mysteries of how God works. But although there are stressful elements, there is the assurance that God will never allow an event to overwhelm us. This is confirmed in 2 Peter 3:9: 'The Lord is not slow in keeping his promise, as some understand slowness, He is patient ... not wanting anyone to perish' (NIV).

Most importantly, God also gives simultaneous responses to prayers when there is need, as seen in Daisy's experience. But we reap the benefits of God's power in coping with disaster when we passionately and unreservedly rely on the power and generosity of God. Through this reliance we affirm with gratitude that 'God is our refuge and strength, a very present help in the midst of trouble' (Psalm 46:1).

References

Anderson, M. B. (1994) 'Understanding the disaster development continuum: gender analysis is the essential tool', in B. Walker (ed.), *Women and Emergencies*, UK: Oxfam.

Anderson, M. B. and Woodrow, P. J. (1989) *Rising from the Ashes: Development Strategies in Times of Disaster*, Boulder and San Francisco: Westview Press.

Barnes, V. C. (2000) 'The Montserrat Volcanic Disaster: A Study of Meaning, Psycho-social Effects, Coping and Intervention', unpublished thesis, University of Birmingham.

Chemtob, C. (1996) 'Post-traumatic stress disorder, trauma and culture', in F. L. Mak and C. C. Nadelson (eds), *International Review of Psychiatry*, Vol. 2, No. 2, American Psychiatrists Association.

George, S. (1992) *The Debt Boomerang: The Debt Harms Us All*, London: Pluto Press.

Jackins, H. (1978) *The Human Side of Human Beings: The Theory of Re-evaluation Counseling*, Seattle: Rational Island Publishers.

Jackins, H. (1982) *Fundamentals of Co-counseling Manual* (Third Revised Edition), Seattle: Rational Island Publishers.

Lima, B. R. and Pai, S. (1993) 'Response to the psychological consequences of disasters in Latin America', 3rd Congress of the World Association for Psycho-social Rehabilitation in Barcelona, Spain, 1991, *International Journal of Mental Health*.

Lima, B. R., Chavez, H., Samaniego, N. and Pompei, M.S. (1993) 'Emotional distress victims: a follow-up study', *Journal of Nervous and Mental Disease*, Vol. 181, No. 6.

Pennebaker, J. W. (1990) *Opening Up: The Healing Powers of Confiding in Others*, New York: Morrow.

Pennebaker, J. W. and Harber, K. D. (1993) 'A social stage model of collective coping: the Loma Preita earthquake and the Persian Gulf War', *Journal of Social Issues*, Vol. 49, No. 4.

Shelby, J. and Tredinnick, M. G. (1996) 'Crisis intervention with survivors of natural disaster: lessons from Hurricane Andrew', *Journal of Counseling and Development*, Vol. 73, No. 5.

Walker, B. (1994) (ed.), *Women and Emergencies*, UK: Oxfam.

WHY WRITE? REFLECTIONS THROUGH PRAYER

Hyacinth Sweeney is Caribbean British from Slough, England. She studied Theology at the University of Birmingham. She has been writing for many years and has had her work published in anthologies, with her first solo publication in 1999. Her aim is to liberate people from mental oppression and to enhance universal empowerment and justice throughout the world, through her words.

In memory of Jillian Brown

When I was asked by a friend to write an article for a book, she sent me the details and I looked through the list of suggested titles. When we met I explained that I was unable to write around any of the suggested titles, for the only thing that comes to mind at the moment is poetry. Her reply was 'Well then, write about poetry and why you write it.' Immediately my mind began to buzz with this idea: Why do I write? What sort of things inspire me? What do I write about and in what style? With this in mind, I sent the forms back and then set about working through the ideas in my mind before I put my pen to paper.

> I remind you to fan into flame the gift of God which is in you through the laying on of my hands. For God did not give us a spirit of timidity, but a spirit of power, of love and of self-discipline. (2 Timothy 1:7)

I would like to explore within this chapter the things that make me write. I would like to fan the flames of the gift that I have been given and expand them more by sharing with you the reasons why I do what I do. I believe that the pen can be quite sharp when it is led in the right way. I have found that my way is through the use of my pen creatively. Before and during the time

I am writing, I always ask God to guide me and give me the wisdom to write the right words.

Why do I write?

Often I have found that I write when I have just experienced something, whether it has happened to me personally or someone else. Over the years I have recorded many incidents that I have seen or stories that other people have told me. I have found that these accounts have received the biggest impact when I have shared them. I must admit this response surprised me, for I felt that I was only expressing how the account made me feel.

Usually, I would sit with pen and paper in hand in deep thought and wait for God to work in me. On many occasions I have been asked to write something on a given theme. When this happens I usually investigate the theme, to see what other people, ancestors for example, have said about it before I begin to write. Sometimes my head is full of information so that I can't wait to get the chance to write it down. At other times, if something very significant has taken place, then I write a lot or keep going until my pen dries up.

Soon after sending back my agreement form my friend died and I lost my enthusiasm to write. Nothing in this world could have prepared me for this predicament and no one could get me out of it. All I could do was to hold on, and slowly move inch by inch forward, until such time that I was not so angry, and my thoughts had become clear again. During this time I prayed a lot – every minute of the day in fact – for I needed to try and understand what had happened and work out how to deal with it. I was so angry inside, but I did not know with who. As the weeks went by my anger changed and I began to have periods of deep thought. On 7 December 1999 I was feeling quite solemn for most of the day, keeping to myself. In the evening I wrote a prayer about my feelings around the death of my friend.

Shattered Dreams

I feel so tired, physically and mentally.
I feel I can't keep up, with all the rushing around me.
My body just aches and longs to be asleep.
But even that's not refreshing, when I wake from my dreams.
I'm tired of smiling when I feel so low.
I'm tired of pretending and just want to show,
the true pain that I feel, for my friend who died.
I just want to cry out and let the world know,
just how I feel and how I can't let go.
Of that sick and twisted feeling,
inside my stomach, and my heart.
The deepening heaviness that is tearing me apart.
To the world outside, I'm as fine, as can be.
But to those inside, I have Shattered Dreams.[1]

It describes how I am really feeling deep inside – the raw pain, loss and fear that only God can see – and not the camouflage 'I'm okay, I'm fine' which everyone was greeted with.

So why did I write this? Well, I needed to express the pain, the loss and the fear that I felt inside in a meaningful way. I needed to let others know what was really going on inside of me. After writing it, the question I asked myself was, will anyone see the prayer, as it's so personal? I saw it as a cry for help and recognition, but also about personal space. A few months later I felt that there was a need to share my thoughts and let those around me understand what I was going through. I also felt that I might not be the only one feeling this way, and maybe my words would be a release to others who were feeling the same, or even to those who could not get their feelings into words. So I wrote again about the loss, the pain and the fear that death brings about.

The L, P, F, of Life

Death is painful to endure
the loss, the pain, the fear.
Death is painfully endured
but time will make amends.

The loss of a person
is indescribable by far.
No words can be a comfort
no words can make a cure.
The loss of a loved one
is inconsolable.
No tears can bring them back
only memories from afar.

Death is painful to endure
the pain, the fear, the loss.

The pain comes from deep within
and knots you up inside.
Your twisted frame is weakened
your mind is insecure.
The pain feels like it will never end,
but it will go away in time.
You'll be strong in body, mind and soul
You will mend again.

Death is painful to endure
the fear, the loss, the pain.

The fear that you may go as well
is thought by one and all.
How will you cope without them,
how will you face next week.
The fear, of being alone now,
without them to share your thoughts.

> But remember their spirit is within you,
> and you can never wipe that out.
>
> Death is painful to endure
> the loss, the pain, the fear.
> Death is painfully endured
> as time, will make amends.[2]

What sorts of things inspire me? In my research I have found that there are many things that can inspire us to write. I have also found that many people follow similar patterns for writing. There are so many things that can inspire you – from what you see around you, to what you feel inside; your close friends and colleagues; a situation in another part of the world, to one within your own country or community and also your own family. Some people may be inspired by the way a baby makes its noises or how a tree blows in the wind; or maybe a photograph of an animal or an object. So many things can inspire you to write, even when you think that you cannot do it.

At church, many members are asked at times to write a prayer. They may struggle and find it difficult to do, maybe because they have never been asked before. But the end result, no matter how long or short, is an achievement to be treasured, because it is your words, and you deliver it to the people. It does not really matter if you end up choosing it from a book, the fact is that you chose it because you felt that it was appropriate for that time and occasion.

If we look at the situations around the world, we will have a basket of options with many different menus to choose from. As a writer I can only write about what I see or what I am told and sometimes even then the words do not come or they may be too painful to place on the paper and so I give them to God in prayer. For example, when I see or hear about something that makes me angry and/or disgusted, I try to write down exactly how I feel. I wrote this account after reading such an article:

After attending a meeting in London, I was sitting in a coffee bar at the station waiting for my train when I read an article that disturbed me very much. After reading it I asked myself 'Why does religion have to lead to murder?' In this article an estranged wife had to flee the country because her husband proclaimed that he was going to slit the throat of their child, because she was not going to bring the child up under the teachings of his religion. The wife had joined her parents who were of a different religion after the break-up of her marriage. The husband's proclamation became reality and he not only killed the baby, but the wife and the parents as well. I read this article in deep shock as I could not get my mind around the fact that this whole family was now dead because of one person's infatuation with their religion. God, our creator, did not make us to kill each other. We are here as a celebration of creation and the sooner we all realize this the better off we all will be. I believe that God made us all different for many, many reasons, but most definitely not so that we can kill each other because we do not like the other person's religion. However, if we look at all of the conflicts over the world over the centuries, 'religion' plays a major part. Even in the religious texts war, killing and fighting can be found at every turn and it is seen as divine – 'God is with us' and 'God be with you' – but is this right, I ask myself. Why should God be a part of us trying to kill each other off?' Is this a part of some plan that we do not know about or is it just that we know no better? Our creator gave us the free will to choose our own destiny, but does that mean that we implicate others in the process? How we choose to live our life is our own affair and therefore we should not involve anyone else with our decision, especially when it involves bringing harm to them.

Prayerful reflection on this behaviour leads me to respond with the following poem.

Define my own destiny

I've made up my mind
To spend some time
To define, my own destiny.

I'll give my self to my Lord
and follow the sacred words
and live, with love in my soul!
and so define my own destiny.
I've made up my mind
To spend some time
To define, my own destiny.

For each day that I live
I promise to give,
my heart, to my God
and so define my own destiny.
I've made up my mind
To spend some time
To define, my own destiny.

Every moment that I live
let it be filled with positive,
affirmations for all my foes
continually defining my own destiny.
I've made up my mind
To spend some time
To define, my own destiny.

When I rise from my sleep
and face the world with my feet.
Be forever at my side
whilst I define my own destiny.
I've made up my mind
To spend some time
To define, my own destiny.

Once I return to bed at night
and close my eyes real tight.
Give me peace throughout the night
to keep defining my own destiny.
I've made up my mind
To spend some time
To define, my own destiny.

In my life let me find
my own peace of heart and mind.
As I've made up my mind
and I will spend my time
defining my own destiny.[3]

Defining your own destiny may involve others in a spiritual way which will allow you to grow, but when it involves violating their very existence then you have a problem. The husband in the article that I read truly believed that he was right. But taking a life, or lives in this case, is wrong in all religions and this needs to be addressed.[4]

While I was at college I used to notice how the black women would be struggling on and off the buses with the heavy shopping bags and trailing children. Looking at them, many of whom looked unwell, overweight, over-stressed and over-worked, made me feel bad to think that this is what we allow our mothers, grandmothers and aunts to become. And yet I also know that if you ever asked them how they felt, they would say 'Oh . . . it's all right' and carry on in the same manner. Sometimes you ask and may even beg for them to slow down, but they will carry on in the same way because now they are so used to it that anything different would not feel right.

When I pray for the plight of black women, I write:

Black Women who make our world . . .

> Carrying the burdens of our world,
> Supporting the men with their woes,
> Supporting the children until they are old,
> Facing oppression at ever' turn.
> Black women you make our world.
>
> Carrying our cares upon your shoulders,
> Taking on board the things you ought not,
> Shopping until you are fit to drop,
> But still mustin' up food for us lot.
> Black women the makers of our world.[5]

Black women make up much of our world and they need to be respected more than they are at present, for without them none of us would be here today.

I find that I write about things that are important to me; things that have a deep meaning to me on many different levels, and prayer focuses my mind. Another example: after a lecture in which I had delivered a paper, I returned to my host's house and we sat in the lounge talking about the evening and how well it was received. We also shared a little about each other's backgrounds. During the conversation she shared a story that had been troubling her for many years now. She really did not know where to go from here, but she also knew that we could not really give her a solution. I believe that all that was needed that night was for her to share the situation, as it was playing on her mind. I also realized that it was not the first time that I had heard a story like this. I felt that there was a need to get this kind of story out into the open so that other people could know what was taking place. However, the last thing that was needed was for someone to have their 'laundry aired in public'. So I continued to talk to God about what was the best way forward for me. I realized what was needed was an opportunity for the victim or victims to speak out. The person to whom harm had been done, put on, needed a voice. On this note I was able to write. It was as if God was allowing me time to work out in my mind exactly what had to be written.

Let it all out!!!

Everything that you remember,
no matter how big,
no matter how small,
Let it out!

Whether it is by pen and paper,
or your own-recorded voice.
Let it out!

Place yourself in front of the camera,
tell the world who you really are.
Put your story in the newspapers and,
Let it all out!

Put yourself behind the screen,
and show the world what you have seen.
Don't let the oppressor, the abuser, the loser,
have the chance to get away any longer.
Let it all out!

Give yourself a chance to tell your story,
while enabling others to tell their story.
So just, Let it all out! [6]

In this example I felt that I needed to write on behalf of someone else, because I had found a way of expressing myself which, at that time as I understood it, they had not. This is not to say that I can do this for everyone, or even want to. The reasons why we write, I believe, are more to do with a personal reaction to the subject at hand or the experience that is received, as God through prayer and contemplation leads us to write.

Another example of what sort of things inspire me happened when I went to hear a pastor from London preach at a local community centre in Birmingham. Her message was so powerfully deep and fulfilling that it moved me in such a way that I didn't realize at first. That night, around midnight, I was writing and the next night I did the same. The next day I felt like a new person because I could not believe that I was writing again with such vigour. I told my partner and a couple of my friends because I really felt uplifted. It seemed that the enthusiasm to write had come back, but in a different form after going through a difficult patch.

Part of the message that stayed in my mind was about the baggage that we carry around with us and won't let go of. She spoke about our worries; past wrongs that had been done to us by someone that we knew, and wrongs that we had done to others; money problems; hurts and ills; not truly forgiving people or ourselves, and burdens of all kinds that we continually walk around with. The things that we often say that we have 'placed at the foot of the cross', but when we look twenty yards behind us, we are still dragging them along from one place to another. We keep on saying to ourselves 'We won't go there any more' or 'We won't do that or allow that to happen again'; but the next thing we know is that we are back in that same situation all over again.

Currently there is a big interest in books of affirmation and of self-love, this being the starting point, which in turn leads you on to loving others. A lot of these writers speak from a personal standpoint, and I believe that is why they are so successful.[7]

The word that stuck in my mind from the meeting was 'forgiveness'. I began to ponder on this and what it really meant. I remember a conversation that I had with my friend on this subject. We both concluded that we can forgive those who have acknowledged that they have done wrong to us. However, we questioned how to forgive the ones who insist that there is not a problem. We also questioned whether it is to do with the way that they act or even if they pretend that the incident did not take place; or even blame it all on you and say it is your fault that it happened in the first place. We both also felt that we would get to a stage of forgiveness, but could not see how we could or even would want to forget the oppressive and unjust stories and accounts with which our lives are so entrenched. We needed a strategy to work this through, and we did not have one.

As a writer of poems and prayers I had found a way of expressing what I felt through my pen. But how did I write down things that I did not want people to know about? Poetry can be a world of secret codes. For example, you can write something and it will have one meaning to the author and a completely different meaning to the reader, who may have experienced the same thing. What this means is that a poem or prayer can speak differently to different people. For me, this night, the pastor's message on forgiveness not only reminded me of the conversation with my friend, but it highlighted its incompleteness. This incompleteness meant that the burden of unforgiveness that I carried was weighing me down. I needed to get rid of it, by placing it somewhere and moving on. The underlying question was, why was I still carrying it around? It was simple: I could not bring myself to forgive someone when they had not acknowledged that they had done something wrong. Furthermore, after all these years, who would believe that this was such a big issue for me, and why did I not mention it before? Well, the answers were quite clear – 'You do not rock the boat unless you can see yourself coming out on top.' However, now that I am older and wiser, I can see the fallacy behind this kind of ideology. Again through prayer, I write:

I forgive them . . .

You may not know the wrongs that you've done me.
You may not even care.
You may not realize the pain that you've caused me,
even though you were there.
But on this day I must release myself,
from this fear that I have trapped inside.
And on my knees I want to just say to my God.
Let me forgive them before I die.

You gave me pain when I was twelve,
but you did not stop right there.

You carried on with your evil ways,
and you didn't seem to care.
And as a child I took the blame
which saved you from despair.
And now I'm grown and know the truth,
you pretend, 'it' wasn't there.
But on this day I must release myself
from all this fear inside.
And on my knees I just want to ask my God.
Let me forgive them before I die.

For many years you've controlled my life,
both near and far from me.
For when I hear that you're coming back,
the fear wells up in me.
For I hate all roads you walk on,
and even the air you breathe about.
I'm mentally sick when near you,
and in my mind, you make me want to shout.
So I need to release my fears from inside,
and fall to my knees and pray.
'Lord God, let me forgive these two people,
before my dying day.' [8]

Through my work experience with young people I have gained many stories and accounts with which my writings are full. Some stories are painful and personal, and to these I have given a lot of prayer. I felt that as an older person now, I should speak out for the people who have been and are still being treated unjustly by society – whether it is society at large or within their own homes by their own family and friends. Many of them cannot speak out, for they do not know how to, or are afraid to. I believe that I have found an outlet and therefore I am using it in the best way I know. I do not say that it will help everyone, but if it helps someone to find their own way of expressing themselves, then I have achieved something.

Forgive them . . . for they know not what they do

For all the times that you hurt me
For all the things that I didn't see
For all the fear that you've put inside
For all the wrongs you've left behind
For all the things that I believed
For all the truths I did not see.
I'll give you to the Lord my saviour
You need to take forgiveness in
and consecrate your life.
To help you see the wrongs you've done me
and give me back my life.

Oh Lord help me get through this pain.
Oh Lord help me always to remain
Forever faithful to your Word
and continue to be part, of my whole world.
For you lift me up when in despair
and when I'm lonely and do not care.
You're the one who tells me to
forgive them, all.

You took my childhood away from me
You made me feel so incomplete
You allowed me to hide, behind a mask
Which made the evil last and last.
You did not care if your friends knew
Just as long as you did not feel blue.
You need to face the Lord my saviour
To take forgiveness in to you
and consecrate your life.
To help you see the wrongs inside you
he'll give you back your life.

Oh Lord help me get through this pain . . .

People like you, will never see
The damage you do, to people's property.
Carrying on, in your abusive way
Instead of turning to prayer.
You need some inspiration
Through your lies you need some truth.
To make the world a better place
for both me and you.

Oh Lord take us both beyond this pain.
Oh Lord help both of us to regain
the peace that we've lost so long ago
and to know that you'll always love us both.
Keep lifting us up when we're in despair
and never letting us turn away from prayer.
For you're the one who always says,
forgive them, all. (Rept.)

For you're the one who always says,
forgive them, all.[9]

With these types of poetry some people may say, on reading them, that I have not gone far enough and that I should maybe 'name and shame'. But as my work is a combination of events it would be improper, as well as impractical, for me to do that. Also, for me the art of forgiveness that I am working on at the moment is a redemptive one.[10] I am forgiving myself for making myself the victim of my own vengeance towards those who have done wrong to me and others, and who have not acknowledged it. I have placed them into God's hands for I do not need to deal with that at the moment. In the future, whether that is near or far, God will let me know what, if anything, I need to do next.

The way in which I write

This is dependent upon the way that I am feeling and what sort of impact that I am looking for. I not only go for an audible sound and expression, but also a visual one. I often jazz up my poems and prayers with different fonts and font sizes, placing borders around them, centring or staggering the verses. I also use particular phrases throughout to gain familiarity and sometimes I may make slight changes to instil new emphases. This, I feel, adds depth and diversity to my writing and also makes it more enjoyable to read and perform. All of this comes to me quite naturally, without the aid of study books on writing poetry and prayer. When I did read up on writing poetry, I found that most of the things that I do have long names attached to them, making them ever so complicated. All of this comes naturally to me and I only found out that each style has a particular name in the writing circles after I had been writing like this for many years.

I have found that within the black community are many talents, but they are hidden from outside eyes. It was not until 1994 that I shared my work openly. I had been writing since my early school days, twenty years earlier. The six years that I spent in Birmingham have allowed me to become more fluent and given me space to try my hand at different schemes, some of which I found easier than others. But what I have noticed is how many other black people, especially women, within the churches hide away their talents. This area of expertise needs to be aired and celebrated by all, and should not be left in the cupboard or in the back of drawers any longer.

After I came to Birmingham and got one of my poems published, I found that my mother was writing prayers for Sunday School, and my sister was writing stories. These two people had never done this before to my knowledge; however, they found that since I had got some recognition, they too felt that they could share their work with me and so it came 'out of the woodwork'. Many other women began to do this and I felt quiet inadequate because I was no expert – I just put down onto paper what I felt. They seem to find something in my work that they could relate to and share openly with me. I realized that I too had done the same back in 1994 with my friend, for if it were not for her, my work would have never got into the public arena. I therefore wrote this poem for her:

Guilty for loving you

In November 1996 my world was in a twist,
you were leaving and I realized,
how much you would be missed.
I'd found a friend,
who could be with me until the end,
and I really didn't want to lose you.

I've kept my distance so far
and admired you as you were.
Coping with all that we gave you.
Never realizing what you really meant,
to someone who had never had,
a friendship of this nature.

As the years rolled on by
we began to have more fun and time
which others wanted to dismember.
They try so hard to pull us apart
by dating us two at a time.
But ended up, just making us go against them.

We'd go everywhere together
sharing our loves and adventures,
some of which were not to be repeated.
We knew each other deeply
and could feel each other's feelings,
and so comfort each other without speaking.

It was so hard to understand,
when I touch your slender arm,
whilst you slept in the hospital bed.
How you have been taken away,
on that very same day,
when my last words were 'I'll see you later.'

I am so lonely right now
without my friend around about
to phone up and share my inner feelings.
For we knew each other so well
that we both could tell
what the other one was thinking.
That's why I ask my God now,
for strength and great power,
to help me get through this situation.
My friend is gone from the earth
and I won't see her any more
but my love will live on without deviation.

No other could be compared
to the friendship that we shared
in this short time that we spent together.
For you will always be the one
that we will turn to for fun,
when our lives have taken us over.
So if I'm guilty of love, then let us all be a part,
of this wonderful gift that I've mentioned.
For a friendship like this, should never be missed.
but treasured for time and always mentioned.[11]

I would like to close this chapter by giving full acknowledgement to my friend, for without her encouragement and steadfast love I would not be where I am today. My only regret is that she is not here to share with me the continued joy that I get from writing. However, all of this could not be done without careful prayer and guidance from God. For 'without our creator our creativeness will be no more'.

Notes

1 *Gemini* – Flowing Dreams, 7 December 1999. This poem was written two months after my friend had passed away. *Gemini* poetry and reflections are by Hyacinth Sweeney, and are first published here.
2 *Gemini* – Flowing Dreams, 23 January 2000.
3 *Gemini* – Fire of Love, 30 December 1999.

4 *Gemini* – Reflections, 7 March 2000.
5 *Gemini* – Fire of Love, 30 December 1999. This poem is incomplete – it is waiting for more verses to be added.
6 *Gemini* – Fire of Love, 23 November 1999.
7 See Iyanla Vanzant, 1998, bell hooks, 1999, Carleen Brice, 1994; Susan L. Taylor, 1993; as some examples.
8 *Gemini* – Flowing Dreams, 1 December 1999.
9 *Gemini* – Spiritual, 3 December 1999. Adaptation of 'Because you loved me' – 'Up close and personal' album by Celine Dion.
10 R. Beckford, *God of the Rahtid* (unpublished – due for publication autumn 2000) for an in-depth analysis.
11 *Gemini* – Fire of Love, 30 December 1999. Dedicated to Jillian Marie Brown, 30 March 1968 to 7 October 1999.

PRAYER AND FASTING

Carl Smith

Carl and his wife Beverley live in West London, along with their four children, Shardae, Chloe, Corey and Shyan. Carl was born in St Thomas, Jamaica. In 1969, age ten, he joined his parents in England. He was converted in 1978 at the age of nineteen, and in September of that year became a member of the Church of God of Prophecy. At the time of his conversion he was an accomplished athlete, but felt that there was a conflict of interest, so he decided against pursuing a professional career in athletics. Since then he has served under a number of appointments both nationally and regionally. This included a ten-year pastorate in the London area. He is also a BSc honours graduate. Currently, as an evangelist, he has an inter-denominational itinerant ministry in preaching and teaching, supported by sponsorship. He is also engaged in a training and development programme for local churches and young aspiring ministries.

Prayer is the offering up of our desires to God for things agreeable to his will, in the name of Christ, by the help of the Spirit, with confession of our sins, and thankful acknowledgement of his mercies. The biblical concept of prayer is based on the nature of God and humanity. It conveys the idea that God is personal, and hence thinks and wills, and that humanity, created in the image of God, reflects these same abilities. Prayer also expresses the sovereign creatorship of God and the dependent creatureliness of humanity. It also teaches that humanity was made for communion with God. Prayer is, therefore, a natural need of humans.

Biblical prayers include praise, adoration, thanksgiving, confession of sins, and petitions. They are both an individual and a corporate expression of the covenant relationship between God and his people. Jesus himself taught how believers are to approach God, as their heavenly Father (Luke 11:2). He warned against mere formalism in prayer (Matthew 6:5–8). He stressed the spirituality of true prayer, as an expression of faith (Mark 11:20–24). We are to pray in his name (John 14:13, 14). We are to persevere in prayer (Luke 18:1–8). We are to have a forgiving spirit as we pray (Matthew 18:21–35). We are to be practical and direct in our prayers (Luke 11:5–13).

From Luke's account in the book of Acts we see that the early Church was a praying body (Acts 1:14; 2:42; 4:31). Paul also teaches that the Holy Spirit helps us in prayer, both by moving us to prayer, and in assisting us in our praying with groanings which we cannot utter (Romans 8:26). He also teaches that, as well as the Holy Spirit, Christ continues to intercede for us (Romans 8:34). Thus, from those passages we can see that the believer's prayer is prompted and aided by the Spirit of God, and is presented to the Father by the Son who is our advocate and intercessor before him. Therefore, we are, says Paul, to 'come boldly to the throne of grace, that we may obtain mercy and find grace to help in time of need' (Hebrews 4:16, NKJV). Prayer enables us to fully transfer the burden of our souls into God's hands. This then releases in the soul the peace of God, which guards it from fear and anxiety (Philippians 4:6, 7).

Personally, I am in no doubt that God answers prayers, for I have witnessed many personal visitations in the form of answered prayers. I recall one such instance back in early November 1998, when I experienced what I can only describe as a miraculous deliverance. That morning, in my usual manner I began to seek the Lord for help and guidance for the day ahead, but this was to prove to be no ordinary prayer. Suddenly, I began praying with such unction (no doubt prompted by the Spirit) until I felt an extraordinary awareness of God's presence. Unknown to me at the time, God was preparing me for the events of that day. I felt such assurance at the time that I knew God would do something. What that something was, I had no idea.

By the afternoon, following what could only be described as a freak accident involving my car, I realized what the Lord had protected me from. The nature of the accident was such that I could have been seriously injured, or even killed. My car, along with three others, was badly damaged. However, mine was a total loss because it was so badly damaged. Apart from being a little shaken up, no one was hurt in the incident. This has made me realize, more than ever, the need to pray – and to pray expectantly.

I believe the words of this hymn speak volumes with respect to the importance of prayer in the lives of believers. It reminds us that there are times when we needlessly trouble ourselves because we fail to realize 'What a friend we have in Jesus'. The author goes on to say,

> All our sins and griefs to bear!
> What a privilege to carry everything to God in prayer!
> Oh, what peace we often forfeit,
> Oh, what needless pain we bear,
> All because we do not carry everything to God in prayer!

The second verse says,

> Have we trials and temptations?
> Is there trouble anywhere?
> We should never be discouraged, take it to the Lord in prayer:
> Can we find a friend so faithful who will all our sorrows share?
> Jesus knows our every weakness, take it to the Lord in prayer.

The third verse continues,

> Are we weak and heavy laden, cumbered with a load of care?
> Precious Saviour, still our refuge; take it to the Lord in prayer:
> Do thy friends despise, forsake thee?
> Take it to the Lord in prayer;
> In His arms He will take and shield thee;
> Thou wilt find a solace there.

Prayer encourages steadfastness and guards against discouragement. In fact, it is so vital that we cannot survive without it. Such is the importance of persevering in prayer that Luke, in his editorial note on Jesus' parable, says, 'Then he spoke a parable to them, that men always ought to pray and not lose heart' (18:1ff., NKJV).

In the light of Luke's statement, it is apparent that a life of prayer does not come easily. Many Christians grieve to admit that, after many years, they still have to force themselves to pray. New believers, mature believers, pastors, evangelists – no group is exempt. Many great leaders would be embarrassed to admit their lack of success with prayer. So it is with most of us. We know that prayer is one of the greatest blessings God offers, but we also know that it is a source of much frustration and guilt. Nevertheless, stories that tell of dramatic answers to prayer set our hearts yearning for the same. However, such fulfilment seems to come to only a few. The rest of us, crippled by frustration, simply put prayer out of our lives. Sometimes overcrowded schedules and demanding responsibilities push conversation with God into the dark and dusty corners of our lives. When we slip in a word of prayer now and then, we cannot help but sense how shallow it is. This harsh reality raises a number of questions: Can Christians hope to experience the blessings of prayer more fully? Can their prayers ever become more like what God wants them to be? What is the problem with our prayers? Where we look for answers to these questions will determine the level and quality of the many riches of prayer.

First, where do we go for help? Because God's word is our guide in all matters of faith and life, we look in the Bible for solutions to our problems with prayer (in a multitude of counsellors there is safety). Immediately our hearts turn to the Lord's Prayer or a few passages in the New Testament, but the Bible has much more to say about prayer than this. The Old Testament Psalms, for example, contain more prayers than any other portion of scripture. They comprise a collection of inspired prayers that God's people sang and recited in all kinds of circumstances: during worship, while travelling along the road, and in the daily activities of life at home. They project the full range of human emotions, from exuberant joy to frantic despair. Sadly, believers often ignore the Psalms and many other passages in which the Bible teaches us how to pray.

As I have said above, from a biblical point of view, prayer may be defined as a believer's *communication with God*. This definition suggests three main elements in prayer: *God, the believer,* and *the communication*. If one of these components is missing, prayer cannot occur. Without God, there is no one to listen to our prayers; without the believer, no one speaks to God; without communication, nothing is said. These three elements will move us toward a more vibrant, fruitful and fulfilling prayer life. Ignoring any one of them paralyses prayer.

The first element of prayer is God

I am quite sure that every Christian at one time or another wonders exactly what role God plays in prayer. Scripture teaches that God has many roles. For example, as the Lord and giver of life, God sustains us, making it possible for us to pray. More than this, he forgives sin that would otherwise prevent us from approaching him. Perhaps his most significant role, however, is that he receives our prayers. As the psalmist wrote, 'Hear my prayer, O God; listen to the words of my mouth' (Psalm 54:2, NIV).

All too often, Christians take for granted God's promise to hear prayer. Therefore, believers who think of God primarily as a close personal friend will offer prayers that are very casual and informal. However, if they think of God as the sovereign King of the universe, their prayers will tend to be more formal and reverent. Thus, believers adjust their communication with God to match their perception of him. As our ordinary conversations reflect our attitudes toward the listener, the same is true in prayer. Our thoughts and attitudes about God largely determine how we speak to him. Thus, our concept of God affects every aspect of our prayer life. Many Christians, for instance, are bored with prayer largely because their perception of God is so narrow. It is not surprising, therefore, that we lose interest in prayer when we severely limit our conception of God. By emphasizing one or two of God's characteristics (attributes) to the near exclusion of all the others, we unwittingly reduce him to a two-dimensional, black-and-white picture. Hence, prayer tends to be monotone, colourless and unrewarding. Therefore, if we do not deepen our awareness of God and his many characteristics, our prayers will fall short of their full potential.

The Bible describes God as a mysteriously and wonderfully multifaceted being. He is love, holiness, justice, mercy, beauty, perfection, life and wrath, to name but a few of his characteristics. All of God's attributes reveal different aspects of his personality. Depending on our circumstances, different dimensions of his character will mean more to us than others. Yet, at no time should the Christian be satisfied with a one-sided conception of God. For our prayers to be filled with life and vitality, we must always strive to deepen our awareness of God in all the ways he is revealed in scripture. The Psalms illustrate the importance of focusing on the many sides of God's character. In their prayers, the psalmists mention many attributes of God. In prayer one may focus on his *reliability*:

> To you I will cry, O LORD my Rock; do not be silent to me, Lest, if You *are* silent to me, I become like those who go down to the pit. Hear the voice of my supplications, When I cry to You, When I lift up my hands toward Your holy sanctuary. (Psalm 28:1, 2, NKJV)

Another psalm emphasizes his *strength*:

> I will love You, O LORD, my strength. The LORD is my rock and my fortress and my deliverer; My God, my strength, in whom I will trust; My shield and the horn of my salvation, my stronghold. (Psalm 18:1, 2, NKJV)

Like the psalmists, we should learn to focus on the wondrous qualities of God as we pray. In this way we are, as it were, praying with our eyes on those particular attributes of God that are appropriate to our situation. If we are hurting, we may look upon God's love and thereby experience the easing of our pain. If we are reeling from wrongs done to us, we may focus on God's justice, and so on. Of this first element of prayer, we conclude that a focus on God is essential to prayer. Only as we deepen our understanding and appreciation of God will our communication with him grow in quality and value.

The second element in prayer is the believer

The psalmist declares, 'Hear my prayer, O God; listen to the words of my mouth' (Psalm 54:2, NIV). Prayer emerges from the human mind and heart, but it is God himself who ultimately gives us the ability to pray. However, often we concentrate on everything except clearly expressing what is deep within us. This shows how little we know about ourselves and how poorly we express what we do know! Self-understanding and self-expression are fundamental to all fruitful communication. The more aware we are of ourselves, the more sincere our prayers will become. The psalmists were deeply aware of their own thoughts and attitudes in prayer. At times, they express jubilation: 'Praise the Lord. Praise the Lord, O my soul' (Psalm 146:1, NIV). Sometimes they present strong desires:

> All my longings lie open before you, O LORD; my sighing is not hidden from you. My heart pounds, my strength fails me; even the light has gone from my eyes. (Psalm 38:9–10, NIV)

At other times, they even admit to deep discouragement:

> My God, my God, why have you forsaken me? Why are you so far from saving me, so far from the words of my groaning? O my God, I cry out by day, but you do not answer, by night, and am not silent. (Psalm 22:1–2, NIV)

These examples illustrate how self-awareness can add a profound dimension to prayer. We must thoroughly assess what is going on within us by asking ourselves: How do I feel? What am I thinking? What are my attitudes, ideas and circumstances? These questions are fundamental to a proper understanding of ourselves as God sees us. Daily, people involve themselves in varying degrees of conversations. At times, these conversations are prefaced with superficial responses such as, 'How are you?' 'Just fine, OK!' We make these exchanges out of polite custom, with little concern for sincerity. However, at other times, when we sense the magnitude of a situation, we feel the need to search inside ourselves and to express our more profound feelings. These are the times when we know empty clichés are inappropriate. Superficial conversation may suffice for some situations, but weighty and personal matters require words that flow from the heart.

This raises the question, 'Do our prayers arise from our hearts?' Often Christians utter one trite phrase after another when praying. It seems that, more often than not, most Christians mimic prayers they have heard even if they do not express their own thoughts or feelings. In fact, many Christians would be surprised and even shocked to hear a prayer expressing attitudes of sorrow and severe disappointment. Instead, we expect a series of pious phrases that will get us safely through those well-rehearsed prayers, which have become a ritual. Unfortunately, more often than not, our attitude in prayer achieves far less than what we anticipate from God. Therefore, if believers want to establish deep, personal contact with God, they must forsake superficial prayer. Like the psalmists, we must examine and express ourselves as honestly and completely as possible.

The third element in prayer is communication

Christians must be conscious of their words when they pray. The psalmist makes this clear: 'listen to the words of my mouth' (Psalm 54:2). No doubt, words are unable to express all that is in our hearts. However, at such times we can take comfort in knowing that the Spirit understands us and intercedes on our behalf. In other words, it is the sovereign work of the Spirit of God to make known the true disposition of the heart:

> Likewise the Spirit also helps in our weaknesses. For we do not know what we should pray for as we ought, but the Spirit Himself makes intercession for us with groanings which cannot be uttered. Now he who searches the hearts knows what the mind of the Spirit is, because He makes intercession for the saints according to the will of God. (Romans 8:26, 27, NKJV)

Despite the Spirit's work, however, we should be very concerned with our words; for words will either hinder or enhance our communication with God. Whilst we may use a variety of expressions in day-to-day communication, most Christians seldom use much variety when they talk with God. They tend to follow one or two patterns for prayer, no matter what their circumstances or intentions may be. They are:

• Jesus, Others, Yourself (JOY).
• Adoration, Confession, Thanksgiving, Supplication (ACTS).

These models help many Christians, especially new believers, to balance the various parts of prayer. Yet all models are limited in their ability to meet the diverse needs we experience.

Even the Lord's Prayer is not to be used as a strict model for communication with God in all situations. It is more of a topical outline, which covers the whole life of the child of God. It addresses how he or she may approach the heavenly Father with respect to any given situation (Matthew 6:9–13; Luke 11:2–4). Although it is a rich resource for learning how to pray, the Lord's Prayer is only a summary outline, which Jesus gave as a general guide to prayer – not a specific rule. Jesus himself prayed in ways that did not follow precisely the model of the Lord's Prayer (John 17:1–26). Thus, no single model is able to communicate adequately all the concerns of the human heart. It is for this reason Paul says to the saints at Ephesus: 'Pray always with all prayer and supplication in the Spirit, being watchful to this end with all perseverance and supplication for all the saints' (6:18, NKJV).

Again, the Psalms are a rich resource on the variety of prayer, which addresses God as the audience of the believer. We often read, therefore, of the psalmists lifting up praises to God: 'Give thanks to the LORD, for he is good. His love endures for ever' (Psalm 136:1, NIV). They also offer laments to God: 'We are consumed by your anger and terrified by your indignation' (Psalm 90:7, NIV). They often express statements about their inward desires toward God: 'Then will I go to the altar of God, to God, my joy and my delight. I will praise you with the harp, O God, my God' (Psalm 43:4, NIV).

Far from being irreverent, the psalmists also sometimes ask questions: 'Will the Lord reject for ever? Will he never show his favour again?' (Psalm 77:7). Following the examples of the psalmists, Christians should vary the content and form of their prayer according to their circumstances and their responses to them. Therefore, if we learn from the psalmists and other biblical figures and begin to imitate the freedom and creativity of their prayers, then we can expect our communication with God to grow richer and more inspiring by the day.

Fasting

Fasting as a deliberate abstinence from food for religious, cultural, political or health reasons, is a practice found in all societies, cultures and centuries. Virtually every religion in the world practises fasting. Even non-religious people fast for pagan parades of asceticism. No one knows how or where fasting had its beginning. Wherever you go, there is the custom and tradition of fasting. Most people are aware of the Jewish fasts including Yom Kippur, or the Day of Atonement. The Muslims also fast during Ramadan, and the Hindus also practise severe fastings.

Primarily, fasting is the act of voluntarily abstaining partially or completely from all food and drink, as the case may be, for a limited period for moral or religious reasons. In the Old Testament, fasting is a sign of mourning (1 Samuel 31:13; 2 Samuel 1:12), or of repentance (Joel 2:12-13; Nehemiah 9:1-2), or of serious concern before God (Psalm 35:13; 69:10; 109:24; Daniel 9:3). Though there were many occasions of national fasting, only one fast day is prescribed by the law, namely the Day of Atonement (Leviticus 16:23; Numbers 29:7). There was always the danger of fasting degenerating into legal observance. Thus, the prophets' protestations (read Isaiah 58:1-11; Jeremiah 14:12).

The New Testament says very little on the subject. Whilst he fasted at the beginning of his public ministry, Jesus lays no stress on the custom of the day, of fasting twice a week; only that his disciples will fast when he is taken from them. There are two sayings which refer to the practice (Matthew 6:16-18; 9:14-15).

The former recognizes the value of the custom but contrasts the simple and sincere devotion to God and his glory, which is expected of the disciples, with the ostentation and desire for human praise among religious 'show-offs'. The latter indicates that Jesus did not lay down any definitive rules for his disciples concerning fasting. In Acts, however, the Christian community is pictured as fasting and praying on solemn occasions (read Acts 13:2–3; 14:23).

The benefits of fasting
However, more than any other discipline, fasting reveals the things and the desires that control us. Therefore, more than anything else, fasting weakens the grip of the things and desires that controls us. The essence of scriptural fasting lies in the self-humiliation and penitence it expresses. Nevertheless, the precise mode of subduing the flesh to the Spirit, and of expressing sorrow for sin, is left to the conscientious discretion of each person. We have a tendency to cover up what is inside of us with food and other things. Psychologically, that sort of thing is spoken of a lot today, especially about people who have much pain in their lives. We would say they escape or medicate their pain with food. They anaesthetize, numb or desensitize themselves to the hurt inside by eating. This is not a rare, induced technical syndrome, which is unique to a few: we all do it. We all ease our discomfort through some means. Some use food to cover their unhappiness, others by setting their eyes on the things they believe will bring them pleasure and comfort. This is why fasting exposes all of us – especially our pain, our pride, and even our anger!

The psalmist declares, 'I humbled my soul with fasting' (Psalm 35:13, KJV). If pride controls us, it will be revealed almost immediately. Anger, bitterness, jealousy, strife, fear – if they are within us, they will surface during fasting. At first, we may rationalize that our anger is due to our hunger. Nevertheless, if we are true to ourselves we will realize that the spirit of anger is within us. Who or what is your master? 'All things are lawful for me, but all things are not helpful. All things are lawful for me, *but I will not be brought under the power of any*' (1 Corinthians

6:12, NKJV). As I have stated above, fasting releases the grip of things on our lives.

Most Christians rationalize away their need to fast and retreat to the medication of food. Daily, they struggle with such questions, 'If I fast, will I find communion with God sweet enough, and hope in his promises deep enough, not just to cope, but to flourish and rejoice in him?' The apostle Paul says, 'I will not be brought under the power of anything.' Whatever we repeatedly submit ourselves to, whether food, television or even computers, tends to conceal the weakness of our hunger for God. Fasting reveals the measure of the mastery of things over us. In Matthew 4:4 Jesus declares 'It is written, "Man shall not live by bread alone, but by every word that proceeds from the mouth of God."' In Matthew, Jesus discloses the opposite or countermeasures to the mastery of things over our lives: 'Blessed are those who hunger and thirst for righteousness for they shall be filled' (5:6, NKJV).

The general principle in fasting is associated with mourning. Scriptural fasting, however, is an expression of brokenheartedness and desperation, usually over sin or over some danger or some deeply longed-for blessing. Paul also warns that there is a fasting which is the property of 'self-made religion and a self-abasement and severe treatment of the body, but has no value against fleshly indulgence' (Colossians 2:23). In other words, this fasting is a 'willpower religion' that actually stirs up the spiritual pride of the flesh even while attempting to master its physical appetites.

On the other hand, Christian fasts move from a broken and contrite heart and poverty of spirit to a sweet satisfaction in the free mercy of Christ. In other words, fasting elevates the soul to ever-greater desires and enjoyments of God's inexhaustible grace. Christian fasting does not bolster pride, because it rests with childlike contentment in the firmly accomplished justification of God in Christ, even while longing for all the fullness of God possible in this life. Christian fasting brings to maturity the results of what Christ has already done for us and in us. It is not our personal endeavours, but the sovereign operation of the Spirit's fruit. Thus, fasting also recalls 'self-control' as a virtue that can be identified as properly belonging to the fruit of the Spirit. John 6:35 (NKJV): 'I am the bread of life. He who comes to Me shall never hunger, and he who believes in Me shall never thirst.'

Bread or food magnifies the work of God in two ways: first, by being eaten with gratitude for all God's goodness toward us. Second, by being forfeited out of hunger for God himself. When we eat, we taste the emblem of our heavenly food, the bread of life. However, when we fast we say, 'I love the reality above the emblem.' In the heart of the believer, both eating and fasting are forms of worship. Both magnify Christ. Both elevate the heart in grateful yearning to the Giver of all good things. Each has its appointed place, and each has its danger. The danger of eating is that, more often than not, we fall in love with the gift; the danger of fasting is that we may, as so many have done, belittle the gift and glory in the power of our own will.

There is a saying: 'Disillusionment often follows naïve admiration'. In other words, it is dangerous to hold up a person, ministry or church as a model of fasting, since there is none without sin, and all our triumphs are mixed with imperfections. We do well to temper our esteem with acknowledgement that there are hidden faults in every saint, and today's victory is no assurance of tomorrow's holiness. This is simply to caution us against transferring the root of our exultation from the historic word of God written, to the contemporary work of God reported. Fasting helps to shape the course of history.

Read Acts 13:1–4. The situation is that Saul and Barnabas and some of the other leaders in the Church in Antioch were worshipping: ministering to the Lord, and fasting. Judging by what happened, we may assume that the burden of the leadership team in the Church was this: 'Where do we go from here as a church?' They were fasting to seek the leading of the Holy Spirit in the direction of their mission. They were hungry enough for God's leading that they wanted to say it with the hunger of their bodies and not just the hunger of their hearts. From this account, the Lord clearly wants us to see a connection between the worship, prayer and fasting on the one hand and the decisive guidance of the Holy Spirit on the other: 'While they were fasting, the Holy Spirit said . . .' This is a significant biblical precedent for engaging in worship, fasting and prayer in the earnest pursuit of God's will for our lives and the life of the Church. It is almost impossible to overstate the historical importance of that moment in the history of the world. Before this word from the Holy Spirit, there seems to have been no organized mission of the Church beyond the eastern sea-coast of the Mediterranean. Before this, Paul had made no missionary journeys westward to Asia Minor, Greece, Rome or Spain. Before this, Paul had not written any of his letters, which were all a result of his missionary travels, which began here. I believe it is fair to say that God was pleased to make worship, prayer and fasting the launching pad for a mission that would change the course of world history.

These same elements have been employed repeatedly throughout the history of the Jewish nation: for example, in 2 Chronicles 20 the Moabites, Ammonites and Meunites came against Jehoshaphat, the King of Judah. It was a terrifying horde of violent people coming against the people of God. What could the people do? What direction should they turn? Verses 3 to 4 say that Jehoshaphat was afraid and turned his attention to seek the Lord, and proclaimed a fast throughout all Judah. 'So Judah gathered together to seek help from the LORD; they even came from all the cities of Judah to seek the LORD.' So there was a great nationwide fast for divine guidance and deliverance. In the midst of the fasting assembly, according to verses 14 to 15, 'the Spirit of the Lord came upon Jahaziel the priest . . . and he said, "listen, all Judah and the inhabitants of Jerusalem and King Jehoshaphat: thus says the Lord to you, 'Do not fear or be dismayed because of this great multitude, for the battle is not yours but God's.'"' The next day when the people of Judah went out, they found that the people of Moab and Ammon had destroyed one another, and it took Judah three days to gather the spoil.

The fasting of God's people changed the course of history. The stories of God's mighty grace through fasting are many. We could tell the story of Moses on Mount Sinai fasting 40 days as he received the law of God that would not only guide Israel for more than 3,000 years, but would become the foundation of Western culture as we know it. Or we could tell the story of how the Jews fasted for Esther as she risked her life before King Ahasuerus and turned the plot against Israel back on Haman's head (Esther 4:16). Or we could tell the story of Nehemiah's fasting for the sake of his people and the city of God in ruins, so that King Artaxerxes granted him all the help he needed to return and rebuild the walls of Jerusalem (Nehemiah 1:4): not to mention the story of Jonah and the people of Nineveh (Jonah 3:5–10). From this brief sketch, it is clear that prayer and fasting are indispensable disciplines in the Christian life.

Further reading

Mahesh Chavda (1998) *The Hidden Power of Prayer and Fasting*, Destiny Image Publishers.

Dutch sheets (1996) *Intercessory Prayer*, Regal Books.

Jim W. Goll (1997) *The Lost Art of Intercession*, Revival Press.

John Piper (1997) *A Hunger for God*, Inter-Varsity Press.

Derek Prince (1973) *Shaping History Through Prayer and Fasting*, Derek Prince Ministries International.

Derek Prince (1976) *How to Fast Successfully*, Derek Prince Ministries International.